Michigan Mountain Biking

A Guide to Mountain Bike Trails in Michigan

Michigan Mountain Biking

A Guide to Mountain Bike Trails in Michigan

Pat McMonagle

Broken Spoke Publications
3142 Eastwood Court
Boulder, Colorado

First Printing April 1994

Manufactured in the United States of America

Library of Congress Catalog Card Number: 94-70224

ISBN 0-9641141-0-0

The sport of mountain biking involves significant risk of personal injury or death. Riders should understand the inherent risk associated with mountain biking. Use of the trails and areas described in this book are done at the rider's own risk. No one associated with the publication assumes any liability for injuries or accidents through the use of *Michigan Mountain Biking.*

Cover Photo by Vicki Horner

Broken Spoke Publications
3142 Eastwood Court
Boulder, Colorado

 RECYCLED PAPER

 PRINTED WITH SOY INK

To Vicki, who showed me the right path.

To Shannon, Kelly, and Kerri. The memories of their smiles and laughter carried me through the miles.

Table Of Contents

Ride Notes

Introduction

"Physical fitness is the basis for all other forms of excellence."
John F. Kennedy

Welcome to the world of mountain biking in Michigan. Here you will find some of the most enjoyable riding to be found anywhere. Michigan is a deeply forested land of marvelous lakes, rolling hills, sparkling rivers, and lush meadows with vast amounts of public land. All this provides for a tremendous variety of excellent riding.

This book is an accumulation of three seasons of full-time riding. I decided on writing a book after wandering the backroads and searching maps looking for challenging rides. Figuring I wasn't alone, I expanded my research to include rides for every level of rider.

Due to the tremendous number of rides in the lower peninsula, I ran out of time and space in the book to describe any of the rides in the upper peninsula. Look for them in the next edition. If I missed your favorite ride, drop me a line, I'd love to go for a ride.

To get the most from the book, buy a computer for your bike. The odometer on the computer, along with the description of the ride, will allow you to navigate the trails that are not marked.

Always be prepared for anything while riding. Rides change, vandalism occurs, a mistake can be made. I have never been mad at myself for carrying too much water or food on a ride.

There are no maps in the book. I opted for this style because I felt mountain biking should include a sense of adventure. Explore the twotracks and trails that intersect with the trail and discover that I left out some of the best riding. Most of the trails are marked in some manner.

Maps for all the DNR pathways can be received by writing to the following address. Please limit each request to five maps.
Michigan Department of Natural Resources
Forest Management Division
Box 30028
Lansing, MI   48909

Maps on the North Country Trail can be obtained by writing to the following address.
Huron-Manistee National Forest
421 South Mitchell
Cadillac, MI   49601

I enjoy riding loops, so most of the rides in the book fall into this category. Shuttles or "out-and-back" rides cause some logistical problems, so rides of that type described in the book are truly outstanding.

The elevation gain figure in the ride summary is an accumulation of all the climbs on the ride. The number was determined by an altimeter on my bike computer. You can use this number, in combination with the distance of the ride, to get a feel for how much climbing is involved.

I classified the rides into three categories of difficulty. A **Family or Easy** ride is basically flat and can be ridden by any rider who has reasonable control over their bike and understands how to brake. A **Moderate** ride will include some climbs and descents, but nothing too steep. The ride will likely be physically challenging. A **Difficult** ride will include a number of steep climbs and fast descents. Bike handling skills are probably challenged and most riders will be exhausted after the ride.

When you are out enjoying the rides in this book, please remember to **respect the rights of other trail users. Trail closure is occurring in Michigan and across the country. Rude riding styles are not acceptable.** Hit your brakes and let other trail users pass you. Shout a warning out when passing. Make others aware of your presence. Complaints from other trail users filter on to the organizations which govern trail usage and trails get closed to bikers.

One of the easiest things you can do to keep access open to trails is join the Michigan Mountain Biking Association (MMBA), the National Off Road Biking Association (NORBA), or the International Mountain Biking Association (IMBA). Part of your membership fee will go towards efforts to keep trails open, creating new trails and managing existing trails.

An even better thing would be to volunteer some time to trail maintenance, cleaning up a parking area around your favorite trail, or working on creating a new trail. In this time of reduced budgets at the state and federal level for our forests and parks, the burden falls on the users to ensure the lasting beauty of these areas. The real heros of mountain biking are not the top racers that are glamorized in the magazines, they are the volunteers that give up some of their riding time to maintain and develop trails.

While riding any trail, please follow the following IMBA rules:

- Ride on open trails only

- Control your bicycle

- Always yield the trail

- Never spook animals

- Leave no trace

- Plan ahead

"Nature is a part of humanity, and without some awareness and experience of that divine mystery, man ceases to be man."
Henry Beston

Ride Ratings Summary

Easy - Family Rides

Bald Mtn North #2   Bald Mtn South #3   Island Lake #5
MacKenzie #12   Betsie River #17   Lost Lake #18
Hartwick #28   Wakely Lake #29   Mason Tract #30
N. Higgins #31   S. Higgins #32   Rifle River #33
Pine Haven #34

Moderate Rides

Ortonville #1   Bald Mtn North #2   Bald Mtn South #3
Pontiac Lake #4   Brighton #6   Yankee Springs #7
Cannonsburg #8   Hungerford #9   Pine Valley #10
Cadillac #11   Udell Hills #13   High Bridge #14
Sand Lakes #21   Wildwood #24   Shingle Mill #26
Chippewa #27   Hartwick #28   Pine Haven #34

Difficult Rides

Brighton #6   Hungerford #9   Cadillac #11
Red Bridge S. #15   Red Bridge N. #16   Lake Ann #19
Vasa #20   Schuss Mtn #22   Jordan River #23
Rifle River #33

Weekend Travel Ideas

One of the things I truly love to do is enjoy my weekends. After spending a weekend enjoying a favorite activity, I spend Monday telling co-workers about my exploits; Tuesday and Wednesday planning the up-coming weekend; Thursday I pack; and Friday I'm watching the clock, anxious to get on the road.

Mountain biking in Michigan lends itself beautifully to weekend travel, camping, swimming, and a long list of other activities. The following lists some possible ride combinations, so if it is Tuesday or Wednesday, start planning; you need to pack on Thursday!

Easy - Family Rides

#17 Betsie River Pathway & #18 Lost Lake Pathway
#29 Wakely Lake & #30 Mason Tract Pathway
#28 Hartwick Pines SP & #31 North Higgins Lake SP

Moderate Rides

#1 Ortonville SRA & #4 Pontiac Lake SRA
#6 Brighton SRA & #5 Island Lake SRA
#7 Yankee Springs SRA (you'll want to ride it both days)
#11 Cadillac Pathway & #21 Sand Lakes Quiet Area

Difficult Rides

North Country Trail - # 14, #15, & #16
#20 Vasa Pathway & #19 Lake Ann Pathway
#22 Schuss Mountain & #23 Jordan River Pathway

Ride Notes

Ride Reference Map

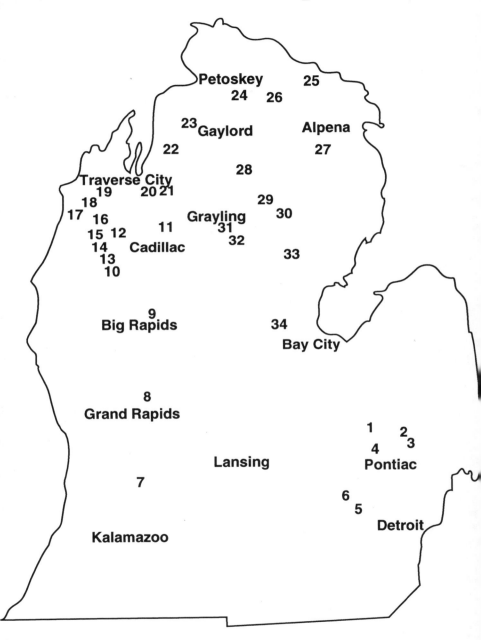

Ride Notes

1 Ortonville Recreation Area

Type:	Loop
Distance:	5 miles
Time:	30 to 90 minutes
Trail Type:	Mixture of singletrack and twotrack
Elevation Gain:	250 feet
Difficulty:	Moderate
Location:	Oakland County
Comments:	A short, fast, fun ride. This is a great place to get away from the crowds.

If you're tired of passing or being passed at Pontiac Lake Recreation Area, take the short drive north to Ortonville and try this ride. You'll find the trail is clear, firm, and not too technical. Rolling hills dominate the terrain that is covered with tall hardwoods. Wildflowers are abundant in the meadows. A few good climbs and quick, thrilling descents will bring riders back again and again. Camping and swimming are available in the Recreation Area.

The trail is located northeast of Ortonville. Turn right on Oakwood Road from M-15. After about one mile, turn left on Sands Road. After 3/4 mile on Sands Road, go right on State Park Road. The Bloomer Unit #3 is on the left.

The trail is a squashed figure eight. Half of the trail passes through hardwoods with an occasional stand of pines. In the forest, the trail contains a number of climbs, and a few of them are challenging. The descents are fast and thrilling.

The other half of the trail passes through large meadows and stretches of shrubbery. In the open areas, the riding is predominately flat with an occasional hill.

From the trailhead, go right, around the road barrier and onto the twotrack. After .1 mile, go left onto the singletrack. This trail segment is in the center of the figure eight. Go right at the first "T" intersection. At about one mile, go left at another "T" intersection and begin riding the left or upper lobe of the figure eight.

Upon reaching a cedar log cabin, make sure to include a sledding hill loop that is to the west of the cabin. This loop contains two nice climbs and fast descents. After the small sledding hill loop, ride behind the cabin and pick up the singletrack on the left. The next section of riding includes several rolling hills.

After returning to the "T" intersection that was encountered at the one mile mark, go right to ride the second loop. This loop is filled with wildflowers. The grasses in the meadow were over my top-bar, soaking me with the early morning dew. After a long straight section of riding, go right at an intersection and climb into a stand of pines. At a fork near the crest of the hill, go right and complete the climb. From the crest of the hill, enjoy a fast plunge followed by a technical, tree root covered climb. The trail passes through the tall pines before dumping onto a twotrack in an old campground. Go right on the campground road and fly down the twotrack all the way back to the parking area.

2 Bald Mountain Recreation Area North

Type:	Loop
Distance:	7.1 miles
Time:	1 to 2 hours
Trail Type:	Singletrack
Elevation Gain:	300 feet
Difficulty:	Moderate - Easy
Location:	Oakland County
Comments:	This ride provides access to a number of lakes. Challenging hills are included along with long flat sections of riding.

This ride is composed of two loops. The first loop contains a number of rolling hills, some of which are challenging to climb and thrilling to descend. The second loop is predominately flat and great for cruising. Camping and swimming are available in the park.

The rides starts at the intersection of Harmon and Predmore roads, east of Lake Orion.

Leave the parking area via the singletrack leaving to the left. At 1/2 mile, Point 3 is encountered. Go left to include a longer loop and the sledding hill, the crest of which offers a great vista. While descending the sledding hill, be cautious. A creek cuts through the trail at the base of the hill. This obstacle offers a great chance for a header after planting a front tire in the depression caused by the creek.

Leaving the overlook at the sledding hill, the trail rolls wonderfully through the hardwood forest. The trail includes several sharp turns, so be prepared.

Point 8 is reached just before crossing a dirt road. Go left at the "Y" intersection just across the road and start the second loop. Wide, sweeping turns characterize the riding on this loop. The trail is almost always skirting the edge of a creek, lake, or swamp. The trail might be wet after crossing several bridges and skirting East Graham Lake. After crossing the dirt road again, Point 8 is reached. Go left at the intersection and return to the parking area.

3 Bald Mountain Recreation Area South

Type:	Loop
Distance:	4.5 miles
Time:	30 to 60 minutes
Trail Type:	Singletrack
Elevation Gain:	200 feet
Difficulty:	Moderate - Easy
Location:	Oakland County
Comments:	A fast, firm trail full of rolling hills, surrounded by hardwoods.

A short but fun ride through some beautiful Michigan hardwoods. When the trail is dry, the riding is fast and the hill can be attacked for a great aerobic workout. Camping and swimming are available in the park.

The trailhead is located between Pontiac and Lake Orion on M-24. Turn east on Greenshield Road from M-24. The trailhead is 1/2 mile east of M-24.

The ride is composed of two loops and a connecting spur. Both loops contain rolling hills and a hardpacked, fast trail. None of the climbs or descents are steep, but they seemed nearly continuous. In the wet months, the trail will be muddy.

The back loop is reached after crossing Spring Creek. This loop contains two 1/3 mile spurs as well as the outside loop. The spur trails should definitely be ridden. Several of the turns are tight and occur on the descents. In general, the trail is wide and fast.

After recrossing Spring Creek, the trail continues to roll before flattening out. The return portion of the front loop is fast. The colors in the fall are beautiful along the trail.

4 Pontiac Lake Recreation Area

Type:	Loop
Distance:	9.5 miles
Time:	1 to 2 hours
Trail Type:	Singletrack
Elevation Gain:	500 feet
Difficulty:	Moderate
Location:	Oakland County
Comments:	One of the most popular rides in the state. A well deserved honor.

The Pontiac Lake ride attracts riders from all over southeastern Michigan. The ride is so popular that there is even a Pontiac Lake chapter of the Michigan Mountain Biker's Association. This is a difficult ride. The rolling terrain combined with tree roots and rocks on the firm, hardpacked trail make for some technical riding. Camping and swimming are available in the recreation area.

To reach the recreation area, take M-59 to Williams Lake Road, north. Turn left onto Gale Road from Williams Lake Road. Park in the southwest corner of the beach parking lot.

Leave the trailhead on the singletrack that will soon cross Gale Road. After 1/3 mile, go left off of a twotrack onto the singletrack. The trail climbs steadily for the next 1.5 miles. At 1.8 miles, the trail forks. The left fork goes to an overlook before rejoining the right fork.

Sometime around June of 1993, the trail was changed to eliminate the campground/lake overlook. The descent from the overlook was rough and eroded from too many riders. Most of the steep descents are the same way.

At 2.2 miles, Point 3 is encountered. The left fork is a great, challenging section of riding: rolling terrain, tight turns, narrow tree lined trail, tree roots crossing the trail, and a rock garden. Fantastic! The right fork saves one mile of distance and injuries to less experienced riders. The two forks rejoin at Point 4.

Leaving Point 4, the trail forks again in 100 yards at Point 5. Both forks cross Maceday Road. The right fork leads to a well and another fork in the trail. The left fork at the well rejoins the left fork from Point 5. This fork leads to a new section of trail for 1993. Go right at the well to save about one mile.

The left fork leaving Point 5 crosses the paved Maceday Road. At the first fork after the road, go left. At the second fork, go right. The trail is tight and winding before riding through a wildflower ladened meadow. The trail then passes through a grassy meadow which is top-bar high. The riding is mostly flat and fast.

Leaving the meadow, the trail starts to climb to another overlook. There are two ways to descend the overlook. The first one encountered on Chalmers Hill (named for a local crash specialist) is steep, rutted from too much braking, and eroded. If the descent looks like too much, go a little further on the hill to find a second trail that sidecuts the hill.

The trail drops for nearly 1/2 mile before climbing a couple of eroded, rocky hills. At 6.6 miles, the trail passes a road barrier. About 100 yards past the barrier, go left as the trail forks. The trail passes through a meadow filled with daisies turned towards the morning sun. Leaving the lush meadow, the trail re-enters the hardwoods where it once again starts to roll as it passes a number of small swamps. I had to avoid an algae covered snapping turtle that was travelling between swamps. The turtle was as big as the inside of my rim! This section of riding also includes another smaller rock garden.

At 7.4 miles, the trail passes Point 9. Go right. The next climb is steep and eroded. Look left at the base of the hill to ride a bypass trail. The trail passes another barrier at a 4-way intersection. Go straight.

The trail climbs into a stand of pines and past a noisy rifle range. Leaving the pines, fly down a long series of hills before grunting up one more hill. The trail dumps down onto a dirt road that leads across Gale Road and back to the parking area.

5 Island Lake Recreation Area

Type:	Loops
Distance:	4.5, 7.4, or 14 miles
Time:	1 to 3 hours
Trail Type:	Mixture of singletrack and twotrack
Elevation Gain:	300 feet for the 14 mile loop
Difficulty:	Family - Easy
Location:	Livingston County
Comments:	A great trail for inexperienced riders to test themselves or for everyone that enjoys avoiding hills.

With its proximity to the Detroit metro area, Island Lake is a favorite destination for riders who enjoy flat terrain. This area is a wonderful place for new riders to sample mountain biking on a trail. The terrain is basically flat, but contains a splattering of hills and sharp turns to challenge all levels of riders. The trail is blazed with blue markers and is maintained by the Michigan Mountain Biking Association. Camping and swimming are available in the park.

Island Lake Recreation Area is located south of I-96 on Kensington Road. A ride of 14 miles is too long for most beginning riders so I split the long loop into two shorter rides so that everyone can find a ride to match their energy and time. The trailhead for the long loop is at Kent Lake in the park. The trailhead for the shorter loop is at the Riverbend Picnic Area. The Island Lake loop is the easiest loop. Follow the description of the long loop ride starting at the River Bend Picnic Area.

The river loop contains more advanced riding, with some hills and surprising turns on the steep descents. This ride starts from the River Bend Picnic Area. Take the trail that is to the right of the picnic shelter. This trail crosses the Huron River via an old cement bridge. After 1/4 mile, the trail has a fork. Go right. Follow the description of the trail in the long loop from this fork. When the trail ends into a "T" intersection with Kensington Road, go right. Cross the river and follow the long loop directions starting at 1.2 miles.

The long loop starts at the west end of Kent Lake. The first section of trail is flat. At .6 miles, go right at the fork in the trail. At 1.2 miles, the trail crosses Kensington Road. After riding between a lush meadow and the river, pedal up a hill and enter the hardwood forest.

At 1.5 and 1.6 miles, the trail passes through small parking areas that provide access to the river and a small lake. Both areas contain picnic tables and benches. From 1.6 miles to 2.8 miles, the trail gently climbs and twists through the hardwoods. The turns are nicely spaced and the trail is wide. This is a great place to practice bike handling skills for future rides. At 2.8 miles, the trail merges with a twotrack. After .1 mile, the trail goes right and leaves the twotrack. After riding along the river, the trail merges again with the twotrack. After 50 yards, the singletrack restarts again on the right.

After passing through a stand of pines that form a cool canopy over the trail, watch for a steep, sandy downhill. Pedal through the hardwoods and a large meadow before arriving at the River Bend Picnic Area at 3.7 miles.

Three trails leave the River Bend Picnic Area. Facing the picnic shelter, the righthand trail is the one the long loop just came in on. The middle trail is the start of the river loop. The left trail, which is hidden behind the restrooms, is the start of the Island Lake loop and the continuation of the long loop.

After leaving the picnic area, the trail enters a thickly forested area before merging with a paved recreation area road. Pedal under the railroad bridge and cross the road to continue the trail. This section of the trail parallels the railroad tracks for 1/4 mile before veering right. In this section, the singletrack rides along Spring Mill Creek. At 4.8 miles, pedal across a sandy twotrack before encountering the paved road again. Go left onto the paved road. Ride along the left shoulder of the road for 100 yards before returning to the singletrack that restarts on the left. Pedal through a meadow before reaching the parking area for the Spring Mill Pond.

I had some problems finding the trail in this area. New development has taken place around the pond and the old trail is not passable any more. I went right at the parking area, then left on the paved road past the pond and relocated the trail on the left. The correct trail is the second trail encountered on the left after riding about 1/2 mile on the paved road. I've been told you can ride through the parking area for the pond and pick up a trail that will travel out to the paved road. Either way will lead to the same continuation trail described above.

After relocating the singletrack, the trail is particularly flat. After a sharp righthand turn, the trail plunges down a surprising hill. Two steep climbs follow the descent. Another steep downhill occurs just before reaching the paved road again. Be careful on the descent! Several small tree stumps are in the trail awaiting some careless rider.

Cross the paved road and enjoy a fantastic section of riding. The terrain is still flat, but contains evenly spaced turns to enjoy. Some of the turns are tight, so be wary. The trail forks prior to entering the Placeway Picnic Area. Both forks rejoin in the picnic area.

Leave the picnic area and turn right onto the paved road.
Cross the river and restart the trail on the left. As the trail
leaves the road, it climbs steeply to reach a ridge above the
river. Some trail changes have occurred in the next section as
the trail passes behind the frontier cabin exhibit. The cabins
are a great place to take a break and explore.

At nine miles, a dirt campground access road dissects the trail.
Water is available in the campground. A sharp right turn onto
a twotrack is required just before getting to the entrance for the
Island Lake section of the park. The trail leaves the twotrack,
crosses the paved road and restarts as a singletrack at the
entrance to Island Lake.

The singletrack is flat and open as it runs parallel to the
railroad tracks so go ahead and pick up some speed. After a
sharp left turn, the trail turns sandy, drops suddenly, and
climbs sharply. When the trail forks in a meadow, go right.
Look for a faint spur trail that is to the right of the main trail.
The main trail leads down a heavily eroded, sandy descent.
The spur trail is a better way down the ridge. Pass an
abandoned car and push the bike up a sandy hill.

At 10.9 miles, stop at a three-way intersection. The long loop
trail turns sharply left and continues up the hill. The Island
Lake loop continues straight, crosses a cement bridge, and
returns to the picnic area. The river loop, which just started,
takes the right fork and follows the long loop directions.

The next section of riding is much more advanced. The trail
drops and climbs along the edge of the river. Some of the
turns are on steep descents. Not everyone has made all the

turns, so some erosion has occurred. Here the trail is passing through a beautiful hardwood forest.

After a sharp right turn, the trail drops down and crosses Mann Creek at 11.8 miles. The trail climbs up, away from the creek, as it continues in the shade of the hardwoods. The next 1/2 mile is slightly downhill with more fun, twisting turns. After rolling ever so gently, the trail has two significant drops. The first drop is sandy so be wary. The second drop turns sharply right at the base of the hill - a nice challenge.

At 13 miles, Kensington Road comes into view as the trail comes to a four-way intersection. Go right, climb up onto the road, and cross the river. Those riding the river loop will take the trail on the right. To return to Kent Lake, cross the road and return to the parking area via the 1.2 miles the trail started with.

6 Brighton Recreation Area

> **Type:** Loop
> **Distance:** 6 miles
> **Time:** 30 to 90 minutes
> **Trail Type:** Singletrack with 1/4 mile of dirt road
> **Elevation Gain:** 300 feet
> **Difficulty:** Moderate to Difficult
> **Location:** Livingston County
> **Comments:** A short but challenging ride with several big climbs and thrilling drops.

Riders who enjoy trails that are always either turning, dropping, or climbing will love this ride. Nestled in a forest of oaks and hickories, this ride contains a few of the biggest climbs south of Grayling. The trail is superbly marked and maintained. Camping and swimming are available in the park.

Brighton Recreation Area is located west of Brighton. Take Brighton Road to Chilson Road. Go south on Chilson for about 1.5 miles to Bishop Lake Road. Go east on Bishop Lake Road to the parking area for Bishop Lake.

Two trails start from the trailhead. The Penosha trail and the Kahchin trail. In the language of the Chippewa Indians who lived in the area, the names mean "long" and "short". The Kahchin trail lies totally within the large loop and shares the first .6 miles of trail. It might be a good idea to loosen up in the parking area because the trail starts to challenge right from the start.

The first 1.5 miles of the trail went by so fast I didn't stop to record any comments. The trail was constantly dropping, turning or climbing. Two big drops proceeded a long, somewhat technical climb at around one mile. The first drop occurs about 1/2 mile after leaving the trailhead and includes several erosion control logs. At one mile, the trail is crossed by several tree roots on the climb. The roots are easily avoided, but climb over them and develop some skills that can be used on other rides.

Between one mile and 1.5 miles, the trail rolls as it twists through the forest. Go ahead and get some speed up. At 1.5 miles, take the left fork and descend to Teahen Road. The right fork provides hikers an erosion-proof trail. Go right on the road and pick up the trail across from the steps for the hikers.

Two challenging climbs are encountered at 1.8 and two miles in the thick oak and hickory forest. Both climbs are steep and technical. At 2.4 miles, the trail forks. Go right, drop into a granny gear and climb a lung burning hill. The climb has some loose sand and gravel, an easy switchback, and several tree roots crossing the trail.

At 2.8 miles, go right as the trail forks and climbs another steep hill. The crest of the hill is filled with wildflowers and offers an outstanding vista. The trail forks again here. Go right and follow the trail into the hardwoods, eventually reaching Teahen Road. Go left on the dirt road and fly down the hill. The trail starts again as the road makes a sharp left turn. Look for a singletrack on the right, going uphill along a fence line just before the turn in the road.

After cresting the hill along the fence line, enjoy two excellent drops. The drops include several banked turns, like a luge run, to increase the fun. At 3.6 miles, go right at the fork. More climbing is encountered at about 4.2 miles. The first climb is steep and somewhat sandy. The second climb is not quite as steep, flattens out for a short distance, then climbs again. The effort expended in these climbs is rewarded with a long, straight downhill that took me across a dirt road and back to the trailhead.

Don't stop at the trailhead. Start around the trail again to ride the inner loop. Ride down the big drop at 1/2 mile and turn right at the fork to start the Kahchin loop. The trail climbs gradually for 1/4 mile, then drops for 1/4 mile on a slightly sandy trail before climbing steeply into a meadow. Pedal through the flat meadow. Take the left fork in the trail and return to the Penosha trail, just before crossing the road and returning to the trailhead.

7 Yankee Springs Recreation Area

Type: Loop
Distance: 11.7 miles
Time: 1 to 3 hours
Trail Type: Singletrack
Elevation Gain: 700 feet
Difficulty: Moderate
Location: Barry County
Comments: One of the primo rides in the state.

The Yankee Springs ride is one of the jewels of mountain biking in Michigan. The trail was designed and implemented through the volunteer efforts of dedicated mountain bikers. The trail has a charisma all its own that will bring you back to ride it again and again. Camping and swimming are available in the recreation area.

Leave US-131 at exit 61. Head east on Chief Noonday Road. Turn right onto Yankee Springs Road. The parking area is directly across from the entrance to Deep Lake Rustic Campground.

Ride across Yankee Springs Road and pick up the singletrack 50 yards ahead on your right. The first two miles of the ride are generally flat as the trail rolls through a mixture of clearings and woods. After taking the left fork at 1.4 miles, wind past part of the campground before crossing the campground access road. Point B is across the road.

From Point B, the trail passes more of the campground before rolling into a marked intersection at about 2.3 miles. Turn left here for a much too short three mile loop. After crossing a smooth foot bridge, get ready for one of the best sections of riding in the state. For the next couple of miles the trail made me imagine I was a driver in a grand prix. I was constantly braking, shifting gears, and accelerating through a long series of tight hairpin turns.

Several trails intersect as the trail passes a road barrier. The trail makes a sharp right just past the barrier, then a sharp left in about 20 yards. The terrain starts to roll quite a bit before forking at an intersection designated by a yellow marker. The left fork is a short spur that leads to the Devils Soup Bowl and the return trail. Take the right fork and enjoy a nice, long descent off the ridge. After riding for 3/4 mile, the payback for the long descent is a thigh burning climb over loose gravel and rock.

The terrain continues to climb and drop as the trail passes through a mature maple forest. The excellent singletrack includes a number of sharp turns and sweet descents off a high ridge. The trail forks as it bottoms-out. Take the right fork and enjoy a lung busting climb up a ridge.

As the trail sweeps into a stand of pines, get ready to challenge your bike handling skills again. Generate some speed and send the pines by in a blur. There is no better section of riding in the state!

After a brief reprieve, the trail starts to roll again as it reenters the maple forest. This section of trail includes some big sweeping turns, grand descents, and an erosion proof rubberized trail.

At a "T" intersection, go right and enjoy a fast, sandy drop as the trail passes under some powerlines. Before making two ninety degree left turns, the trail climbs the hill that was descended under the powerlines.

A somewhat confusing four-way intersection is reached shortly after cresting the hill. The problem is that this intersection is marked for both skiing and biking. Signs point to trails that head-off in every direction. Veer left and cross directly under the powerlines. The trail will then veer right and start to climb to the ridge above the Devils Soup Bowl. A number of hiking trails intersect with the singletrack in the area of this unique geological formation. Follow the bike tracks and trail signs and stay off the hiking trails.

The trail is slightly downhill as it leaves the dense forest and meanders through wildflower ladened meadows. After passing just below a road, the trail crosses a small creek and veers left. Expend any remaining energy on yet another fantastic section of trail that eventually dumps out onto the campground road. Truly a great ride. I rode into the campground, filled my water bottles and went around again.

8   Cannonsburg State Game Area

Type:	Loop
Distance:	7 miles
Time:	1 to 2 hours
Trail Type:	Singletrack
Elevation Gain:	300 feet
Difficulty:	Moderate
Location:	Kent County
Comments:	Nice gently rolling ride. Great place for advanced beginners to hone their skills.

This ride offers a little of everything that I would expect from a singletrack ride: quick descents, water crossings, short steep climbs, a series of sharp turns, and some meandering through a forest. The ride is popular for Grand Rapids area bikers. Camp at Yankee Springs and ride the trail there too.

To get to the Game Area, get on M-44 on the northeast edge of Grand Rapids. Take M-44 to Knapp Road and turn right. Follow Knapp for a little more than four miles to Egypt Valley Road. Turn left on Egypt Valley and follow Egypt Valley to 4 Mile Road and turn right. The large parking area is on the right after about 1/2 mile.

Note that the land for the Game Area was purchased with hunter's monies and the area is posted as being closed to riders from September 15 through January 31.

To start the ride from the parking area, ride around the road barrier and pick up the singletrack. After a short distance, the trail forks and crosses a small creek. The left fork is the correct choice here as it uses a foot bridge to cross the creek. However, in the wet months, the right fork is the better alternative. At .3 and .4 miles, ride past two left hand spurs.

At .8 miles, after grunting up a hill, roll downhill through a young oak forest and cross Egypt Creek via a small bridge.

At 1.3 miles, the singletrack ends into 3 Mile Road. Turn left. Ride on the dirt road for .3 miles to the next parking area. The singletrack restarts here and passes through some quick, short rises, and drops for the next mile as the trail twists around and crosses Egypt Creek again via another bridge.

At 2.8 miles, the trail crosses a smaller creek via another bridge and forks. Go right. The left hand fork will lead back toward the parking area to make a shorter loop.

At 3.4 miles the trail offers three choices. The first spur leads to private property and dead ends. The second spur is for gonzo riders who want a technical challenge. This spur goes up a steep hill covered with loose rock. The last spur takes a kinder, gentler approach to the hill. The last two spurs lead to 4 Mile Road which temporarily interrupts the trail. When taking the easier spur, turn left onto the road and ride up the hill to pick up the trail on the right.

After .5 miles, the trail forks again. Go right. After a short climb, expect a nice downhill with some sharp turns. At 4.4 miles, take the sharp left turn as the trail forks. Follow this fork for 1/4 mile and take the right hand fork after climbing a short hill.

At 4.7 miles, a trail merges in from the left and shortly after, another trail forks off in the same direction. Stay to the right. Almost immediately, the trail dumps onto Dursum Road. Turn right. Ride down the hill, pass a small parking area, and pick up the trail on the left. Take the singletrack that runs away from the road.

A spur trail joins from the right at 5.6 miles as the terrain starts to roll. Crank through the last section and take advantage of some of the gears rarely used on the trail. Ride past two left hand spur trails and continue through some slightly sandy riding to a "T" in the trail. Turn left at the intersection and return to the singletrack. The remainder of the trail is flat before returning to the parking area.

9 Hungerford Trail

> **Type:** Loop
> **Distance:** 10 miles
> **Time:** 1 to 4 hours
> **Trail Type:** Mixture of singletrack and twotrack
> **Elevation Gain:** 500 feet
> **Difficulty:** Moderate to Difficult
> **Location:** Newaygo County - Manistee National Forest
> **Comments:** Exciting ride with a number of short challenging climbs and thrilling descents.

Hungerford trail is a cross country ski area located just west of Big Rapids. A favorite of Big Rapids natives, the ride is a nice mixture of singletrack and twotrack in a rolling forest of northern hardwoods, aspens, and pines. The trail is marked with numbered intersections and blue markers. Limited camping is located near the trailhead, and Hungerford Lake offers a pleasant swimming hole.

From Big Rapids, take M-20 west for 8.5 miles to Cypress Avenue, then 1/2 mile north to a cemetery. Turn right on Hungerford Lake Road and proceed for 1/2 mile to Forest Road 5134 and turn left. The trailhead is 1/4 mile ahead on the left.

The trail starts behind the information area and immediately crosses Forest Road 5134. The trail forks twice; go left at both intersections and climb a gentle hill on a small dirt road. At .8 miles is the intersection for Point 1. Veer right onto a gently climbing wide trail. On the descent from this climb, the trail forks and continues on the twotrack going right.

At 1.3 miles the trail forks. Go right and follow the singletrack that rolls into Point 2. At Point 2, the trail veers right and meanders uphill through a fragrant stand of pines. On the descent, the trail crosses a dirt road and turns into a twotrack. This section is flat and sandy in spots as it passes under some powerlines. After a short time, the trail merges into Forest Service Road 5465. Turn left onto the road and ride 70-80 yards before picking up the singletrack on the right. The trail climbs slightly before intersecting with a twotrack. Go right. The twotrack rolls downhill, crosses road 5465 again, and climbs steadily. At the crest of the hill, the trail turns left onto a singletrack and eventually crosses Forest Road 5134. Point 3 is just across this road.

The next stretch of trail is exhilarating. The trail climbs short steep hills and plunges down into some quick, crisp turns as it pops in and out the forest of hardwoods. After 1.3 miles of fun, drop down and cross a twotrack. The singletrack soon merges into a twotrack that skirts the edge of a marsh. At the next "Y" intersection, veer right, and climb two short steep hills before arriving at Point 4.

After finishing the climb, the trail delightfully descends through the hardwoods. A twotrack bisects the singletrack at the bottom of the drops, but just roll past it and continue onto Point 5. At Point 5 the trail forks. If the ride is taking its toll after all the climbing, take the left fork to Point 7 to shave off a couple of tenths of a mile. Otherwise, go right, and continue to Point 6.

After leaving Point 5, the singletrack climbs two short steep hills. Now enjoy some thrilling drops and challenging turns as the trail heads to the intersection at Point 6. At Point 6, pick up the twotrack that leaves to the left. The trail at this point is basically flat. At 7.4 miles, the trail comes into a clearing and veers right onto a singletrack which leads to Point 7.

The trail from Point 7 to Point 8 provides more exciting singletrack riding as it winds and climbs through a stand of pines and plummets down the side of a ridge. The trail crosses several twotracks, but is well marked. Arrive at Point 8 after climbing slightly uphill through some hardwoods.

Shortly after the intersection at Point 8, the trail drops sharply and crosses a road. The trail becomes slightly larger than a singletrack as it slowly climbs a ridge and then descends the other side. The trail is sandy on the descent of the ridge, so be prepared. The trail splits and continues via the left fork. The trail continues to drop as it rolls past a camping area for Hungerford Lake. The lake offers a nice place for a well earned, refreshing swim. The trail gradually climbs back to the trailhead and the parking area.

10 Pine Valley Pathway

Type: Loop
Distance: 6.5 to 8.5 miles
Time: 1 to 2 hours
Trail Type: Mixture of singletrack and twotrack
Elevation Gain: 200 feet
Difficulty: Moderate
Location: Lake County - Pere Marquette State Forest
Comments: Short, pleasant ride that is a great mixture of flats and rolling terrain.

This is a truly enjoyable ride through a beautiful section of forest. This area is just begging to be explored more than what is available on the pathway. Twotracks are abundant and head in nearly every direction. The parking area also serves as the parking area for a motorcycle trail that is somewhat sandy but thrilling to ride.

From Baldwin, go north on M-37 for 13 miles, and turn right on 7 Mile Road. The large parking area for the ride is on the right. Camping and water are available two miles south on M-37. The trail is marked with blue markers and paint spots.

The trail leaves the south end of the parking area, rolls past Point 1 and Point 2, and starts to gently climb. After crossing 7 Mile Road, the wide grassy trail intersects with a twotrack and continues to climb gently. At the bottom of a short hill, the trail leaves the twotrack on the left. The trail rises and drops through a hardwood forest, then enters a stand of small pines before crossing an unnamed dirt road at 1.7 miles.

The bonus for completing the gradual climbs is a pleasantly graded downhill on a singletrack through a deeply forested section of woods. At the bottom of the drop, the trail merges

with a grassy twotrack and begins to get more exciting.
Before crossing 7 Mile Road again, several thrilling downhills
are followed by short, sharp climbs. Shortly after crossing the
road, Point 4 is encountered.

From Point 4 the trail skirts a ridge above Lost Lake and
continues a short distance to Point 5. From Point 5 there are
two choices: turn right and add two miles to the ride by adding
the Point 5-7-8-3-4-5 loop, or continue straight to Point 6. The
extra loop is a pleasant ride and worth exploring. Continue to
Point 6 via a flat section with three forks. Take the right-hand
fork each time.

At Point 6, cross a dirt road that leads to Steward Lake. After
crossing the road and taking the left fork, climb slightly, then
enjoy a long, windy downhill. The fun continues after
crossing a twotrack. The trail climbs, drops, and drops again
as it winds in and out of a northern hardwood forest and a
stand of young aspens. After reentering the hardwoods, the
trail climbs and then drops with all the speed desired into Point
7.

After rolling downhill from Point 7 to Point 8, the trail turns
grassy and passes Little Seyers Lake. While riding along the
tree filled lake, the trail forks right just before a large grassy
clearing. The remainder of the trail meanders through a
younger forest before returning to the parking area.

11   Cadillac Pathway

Type:	Loop
Distance:	9.5 miles
Time:	1 to 2 hours
Trail Type:	Singletrack
Elevation Gain:	500 feet
Difficulty:	Moderate to Difficult
Location:	Wexford County - Pere Marquette State Forest
Comments:	Thrilling ride with consistently rolling hills. No long granny gear grunts, but some long, sweet downhills. A favorite of mine!

I've always skipped this ride when passing through Cadillac in the past, thinking a ride so close to town wouldn't offer much. Big mistake! The contour of the terrain made this ride one of my favorites. Every climb is rewarded with a delightful downhill as the ride twists and turns through the hardwoods. The trail is maintained by the Cadillac Area Teachers Association and is in superb shape. As always, be in control on the descents. There is some loose sand on the trail. Camping is abundant in the area. Swimming is available just off the trail in the Clam River.

From Cadillac, take US-131 north and turn right onto Boon Road. After 3.5 miles, the road takes a sharp left turn and the parking area is on the right.

The trail starts through a stand of pines, and is flat as it quickly passes Point's 2, 3, and 4. After Point 4, get ready for the aerobic challenge, as the well maintained trail starts to roll on its way to Point 8.

At 1.6 miles, after cresting a hill, two trail markers designate

Point 8. Head left and enjoy a great section of riding. The trail climbs, drops, and darts through the hardwoods, which offers all the workout and speed desired. After passing a couple of twotracks, fly past Point 9 and continue to the left.

For the next several miles the trail passes several fitness stations. If the challenge from the rolling hills is not enough, stop at one of these stations.

From Point 9, the fun continues past a gas pipeline and a twotrack, as the trail rolls into a big intersection at Point 10. Go right. Climb and drop repeatedly before passing the pipeline again. The trail then offers a thrilling descent that had my eyes watering as I flew past Point 12.

On the way back to Point 8, the terrain continues to roll as it passes four twotracks. Just before returning to Point 8, a challenging climb made me reconsider riding the loop again.

When leaving Point 8 to return to the parking area, take the left fork at the unmarked "Y" intersection. The trail then offers up a sweet, long downhill and a great flat section. Crank-out here on the hardpacked singletrack. After another downhill, the trail passes a small twotrack and Seeley Road. Point 5 goes by in a blur after climbing and dropping two more sets of hills.

A slight downhill grade, combined with smaller rolling hills, makes the ride into Point 6 tremendous fun. Make a sharp right turn at the trailhead sign and continue. The trail flattens out, rolls in and out of a stand of fragrant pines, and arrives at Point 7.

From Point 7, views of the meandering Clam River are offered.

Passing a nice sandy beach, the trail turns left, crosses the twotrack, and returns to the parking area. The beach area provides a nice spot to swim, relax, and re-create this thrilling ride.

12 MacKenzie National Recreation Trail

Type:	Several loops
Distance:	Variable
Time:	1 hour to all day
Trail Type:	Mixture of singletrack and twotrack
Elevation Gain:	Variable. Few hills or a lot of climbing
Difficulty:	Easy. A couple of trail segments are difficult
Location:	Wexford County - Manistee National Forest
Comments:	Fantastic trail system for a family outing. Challenging terrain for more advanced riders.

The MacKenzie trail is a great place to ride for all skill levels. A cross country ski trail in the winter, the trail consists of several short loops in a marvelous hardwood setting. Advanced riders can attack the more challenging sections. Riders who enjoy flat terrain will enjoy the variety in the loops. The large meadow between Points 15 and 16 is a great place for a picnic. Pack a day-pack full of snacks, ride up to the meadow, and drop off the pack. After some pleasant riding, rendezvous in the meadow before riding some more. Several National Forest campgrounds are in the area.

From Cadillac take M-55 west to Caberfae Road. This drive from Cadillac on M-55 is one of the most scenic stretches of forested highways in Michigan. Take Caberfae Road past the ski area. The parking area is 3/4 mile west of the ski area entrance on road #38.

It would be impossible and unfair for me to describe a single ride on this trail system. The loops are so short and the intersections so frequent, directions would be useless and frustrating. Instead I'll describe several of the trail segments and their characteristics.

The trail consists of four tiers. Each tier has several spur trails that lead up or down to another tier. In general, the riding on each tier is basically flat. The riding "up" to the next highest tier is generally uphill. The gradient is gentle on most of these climbs and is rideable by everyone.

Riding on, and between, the second and third tiers is a great section with several loops and lots of variety. This is a wonderful area for a family or infrequent riders to spend the day. The terrain is gentle and the forest is beautiful. Wildflowers are abundant. The picnic meadow is in the upper left corner of this section.

Riding on the first or lower tier is slightly more advanced. The trail is grassy, slightly uphill (when leaving Point 20), and rough, but definitely rideable.

The upper or forth tier is basically flat with a mixture of singletrack and twotrack. The two center spurs that lead up to the highest tier offer more advanced riding. The trail segment from Point 15 to Point 11 has a steep uphill climb.

The more advanced rider can enjoy the outside loop on the far right of the trail system. This is a nice way for the return journey (or a tough climb up to access the rest of the trail). The trail is slightly downhill but is somewhat grassy and rough. The final section from Point 5 to Point 4 is somewhat difficult to find, but offers a great downhill section with some tight, hair-pin turns.

To get to the four tiers, the trail leaves the parking area on a twotrack and passes through a beautiful stand of pines. At Point 2 the trail forks, giving two options to arrive at Point 3. The easiest way is to go straight along the outside of the stand of pines. The right-hand fork winds through a stand of hardwoods on a singletrack. From Point 3, ride down the hill, across the wide bridge, and uphill to Point 4. The trail forks at Point 4. The right fork leads to the more advanced terrain described above. Continue straight to Point 20 and the first of the four tiers.

13 North Country Trail - Udell Hills

Type:	Out and back
Distance:	11.6 miles
Time:	1.5 to 4 hours
Trail Type:	Mixture of singletrack and twotrack
Elevation Gain:	400 feet
Difficulty:	Moderate
Location:	Manistee County - Manistee National Forest
Comments:	Bike handling skills are tested on this excellent singletrack full of tight, twisting turns.

Don't skip this section of the North Country Trail. The terrain is more moderate than the segments to the north, allowing most experienced riders access to the trail. The long sections of narrow, winding, primo singletrack kept me wide-eyed, alert, and smiling. This segment of the trail does continue on to the Freesoil Road trailhead (22 miles round-trip). I chose not to describe miles six through 11 because the trail was on pavement for a mile (against one of my rules for rides in this book), the riding was flat and "uneventful", the bugs were ferocious, and the last mile was wet. About half a dozen National Forest campgrounds are in the area, many of which include swimming.

The trail starts about one mile east of Udell and five miles west of Wellington on M-55.

This area of forest is mixed with large tracts of private land so the first 1/2 mile of the trail is on Forest Road 5207. Don't be confused, like I was, that the gray diamond blazes are located on the left side of the road and the trail leaves the road to the right. The trail is flat until crossing a twotrack just before reaching the one mile post.

The next eight miles of riding are fantastic. Whether the trail is flat, climbing, or dropping, it is nearly always turning. Some of the turns have trees on both sides of the trail, leaving just enough room to squeeze through. The descents reminded me of picking a line while skiing the steep, tree lined powder bowls of Colorado and Utah.

Leaving mile marker one, the trail climbs and winds, twice crossing an old twotrack before finally merging with it. The twotrack rolls, but climbs steadily through a forest of hardwoods. At 1.9 miles, the trail leaves the twotrack on a singletrack that is on the right.

The decaying leaf-covered singletrack is flat or drops as it twists and turns to the three mile marker. At 2.1 miles, watch for a small clearing in the forest to enjoy a spectacular view to the north.

The great riding continues past mile three. At about 3.7 miles, the trail gradually expands to a twotrack. The trail stays with the twotrack for 1/4 mile then turns sharply right to reach mile marker four. I missed this turn because I was looking up, admiring how big the trees were. The mile between markers three and four was generally flat to gently rolling with more challenging turns.

Leaving mile marker four, the trail drops all the way to mile marker five. No steep drops, but enough of a pitch to make the tight turns even more challenging. Mile marker five is encountered just as the paved road is reached. Turn around and enjoy the return trip.

To continue to the Freesoil Road trailhead, go left on the paved road. After crossing the Pine River, go left at a 4-way

intersection. The singletrack restarts on the right about .4
miles from the intersection.

It is also possible to make a loop out of the ride by using the
twotracks that crisscross through the area. I drove a loop after
riding the area. The twotracks were deeply forested and
packed except for all but 1/2 mile which was sandy. Pick up a
topographical map of the area so as not to get lost.

14 North Country Trail - High Bridge to Dilling Road

Type:	Out and back
Distance:	10 miles
Time:	1 to 2 hours
Trail Type:	Singletrack
Elevation Gain:	300 feet
Difficulty:	Moderate
Location:	Manistee County - Manistee National Forest
Comments:	A spectacularly scenic ride that includes a cruise along the shore of the majestic Manistee River. Expert, technical riders can challenge themselves on a number of switchbacks and steps.

This is a must ride for lovers of river country. The trail skirts the shore of the wide, quick running Manistee River before climbing and offering more river views from a lofty perspective. Tight, twisting, slalom like turns challenge bike handling skills. This out and back ride can easily be combined with the Red Bridge rides to make a full day of riding. Camping is available at Tippy Dam on Dilling Road.

High Bridge is two miles north of M-55, west of Cadillac. The trail starts at the northeast corner of the bridge.

The trail drops slightly from the road and skirts the edge of a forest of cattails. The singletrack climbs away from the wetlands to a hardwood covered ridge above the river. Two wooden bridges are located in the first mile of riding. The first bridge has five steps that come in quick succession. Good practice for technical challenges to come.

The trail climbs gradually after a mile of riding. The trail twists and turns on the ascent. A great section of riding on the return journey! The trail is narrow and includes several sections where a bike can just squeeze through trees that line both sides of the trail. Two miles into the ride, a small clearing offers a panoramic view of the river and surrounding countryside.

The trail descends from the view area through a series of challenging turns before switchbacking right onto a twotrack. Accelerate down the twotrack before turning left onto a singletrack. The singletrack is cut along the top of a dramatic knife's edge ridge. The ridge is short but includes several technical steps to descend and more steep stairs to climb. Mere mortals can push through this short section. The area is rideable.

The twisting trail climbs after leaving the ridge. At about 2.7 miles, another view of the river is available through a break in the hardwoods. The trail is flat before descending a steep ridge. To control erosion on the steep terrain, the trail includes a number of tightly packed switchbacks. Some of the switchbacks are rideable, both on the descent and the climb. Nice place to work on some advanced skills. Common sense goes a long way in this section.

The descent of the ridge leads to a beautiful river valley. Cross a bubbly brook into a beautiful area of wildflowers as the trail angles directly toward the river. As the trail journeys through this gorgeous valley, stop often to spy on strong swimming gamefish fighting the current and large snapping turtles sunning themselves on the deadwood in the river.

Watch for wild strawberries and raspberries as the trail meanders the 1.4 miles through the river valley. A tricky, sharp, righthand turn is required after crossing a noisy creek that is rushing to get to the river.

The trail climbs gradually away from the valley as it enters a stand of hardwoods. After a nice section of flat riding, watch for the lodge of a porcupine in a red oak tree. The lodge is at about 5.1 miles. The trail climbs a short ridge after the lodge before reaching Dilling Road.

The return journey drops much more than it climbs. The twisty turny sections after the knife's edge ridge are outstanding!

15 North Country Trail - Red Bridge South

Type:	Out and back
Distance:	11.6 miles
Time:	2 to 4 hours
Trail Type:	Singletrack
Elevation Gain:	900 feet
Difficulty:	Difficult
Location:	Manistee County - Manistee National Forest
Comments:	A great, narrow singletrack filled with long gradual climbs, flat cruising areas, and exciting downhills.

The Red Bridge South ride contains about half the climbing as the northern route. Strong riders can link the two segments for a 30 mile ride with 2900 feet of climbing. The combined ride is one of my favorites. The south segment is characterized by several sections of trail where trees line both sides of the singletrack, leaving barely enough room to squeeze through. The scars on the trees indicate that not every rider has successfully negotiated these sections. Expect a couple of long grunts to achieve the 900 feet of gain. The trail is blazed with gray diamonds and mileage markers.

The trail is on Coates Highway, 1.25 miles east of Red Bridge. No trailhead sign is found for this section of the trail. Park on Forest Road 5484, 200 yards east of the trail. This description is for the segment that travels south.

The trail climbs 120 feet in the first 1/4 mile, so get loose before climbing on the saddle. A switchback is encountered about 200 yards from the road. After climbing the ridge above the road, the trail flattens out as it passes through a majestic hardwood forest carpeted by ferns. The first mileage marker encountered is mile 10 in this section of the North Country Trail. On the way to this mileage marker, the singletrack includes several of the narrow tree lined sections and erosion control logs.

The trail rolls for a short distance after leaving the mileage marker. On a steep climb, attempt to negotiate several more of the narrow tree lined sections. A challenge! The trail was designed to include the narrow sections to keep motorized vehicles and horses off the trail. At 1.6 miles, watch for a clearing in the trees on the left. Enjoy a beautiful view of the Manistee River.

Leaving the overlook, the trail is sidecut into a steep ridge as it drops for .4 miles. Mile marker 11 is passed on the descent. Bikers have caused substantial erosion problems on the narrow trail on this descent. The wonderful descent ends at the floor of the valley. The trail is flat and fast for 3/4 miles through a beautiful stand of tall maples as it cuts through the valley. One hundred feet of climbing is required in .2 miles to reach mile marker 12.

At approximately three miles, thick vegetation narrows the trail. Look for a tasty snack of wild raspberries in this area. The next section is flat to slightly downhill on a rutted twotrack. Pick up some speed and alternate between the tracks to enjoy the best riding. At 3.6 miles, veer right away from the twotrack onto a singletrack.

The trail rolls past mile marker 13 before turning flat for nearly a mile. Enjoy the scenic cruise through the hardwoods before climbing slightly to mile marker 14. Leaving the mile marker, the singletrack includes a twisting, turning, thrilling descent to the valley floor. A great section of riding that will challenge a rider's bike handling skills.

The remainder of the trail is predominantly flat before reaching Dilling Road. Turn around and enjoy the ride back to Coates Highway.

16 North Country Trail - Red Bridge North

Type:	Out and back
Distance:	18 miles
Time:	3 to 5 hours
Trail Type:	Singletrack
Elevation Gain:	1900 feet
Difficulty:	Difficult
Location:	Manistee County - Manistee National Forest
Comments:	One of the primo rides in the state for advanced riders. A tremendously beautiful area that includes mile long climbs and descents.

The trail is a marvelous singletrack that includes long climbs and relentless drops . None of the climbs are extremely steep, but several are long. One is nearly a mile. As an out and back ride, each sweet descent becomes a challenging climb, each climb a thrilling decent. The setting exceeds the quality of the ride. Camping is available at Tippy Dam, south of the ride.

The trail is on Coates Highway, 1.25 miles east of Red Bridge. There is not a trailhead sign on Coates Highway, so watch for a singletrack that crosses the road. Park on Forest Road 5484, 200 yards east of the trail. This description is for the segment that travels north.

The locals tell me the trail is close to being closed due to trail damage. Damage caused by lazy bikers who prefer to make new trails around erosion control logs instead of riding over the log. Let's work together to keep this fantastic ride open. If the fatigue from the ride is too much, walk your bike up the hills instead of causing trail damage.

The trail climbs gradually for the first 1/2 mile. At the crest of the hill, the forest clears just enough to offer an incredible eastward vista. I made a mental note to come back and ride the trail every fall. But don't wait - in the spring and summer months, the forest is lush and wildflowers are abundant.

The trail surprisingly includes a switchback at about .6 miles. Switchbacks are rare in Michigan, but common in areas with steeper terrain. After a long descent, the climbing starts again. Much of the trail is sidecut into the steep hills. Hence the erosion problems. The forest is so thick that it is not possible to see the bottom of the ridge. Beautiful.

The riding between miles two and three is generally flat. Here the trail is reminiscent of Yankee Springs, with tight, tricky turns to maneuver through. Contact with a couple of trees should be expected somewhere along the ride.

Mile three is entirely downhill! The trail drops magnificently to the valley floor. Care is required on the descent to stay on the narrow trail. If the bike wheel slides off, stop and repair the damage. The forest is so thick, it is almost completely dark on a sunny day at noon.

Mile four climbs approximately 260 feet returning to the ridge. No sections are particularly steep as the trail tests the gluts, thighs, and lungs.

Mile five is mostly flat before dropping again to the valley floor at about 6.5 miles. The descent contains a number of erosion control logs. The trail climbs steadily to mile seven.

Mile seven drops splendidly to cross the clear, fast running Eddington Creek. After crossing the creek via a bridge, the trail is slightly sandy for a short distance. The only such spot on this segment of the North Country Trail.

At about 8.4 miles, another clearing offers a spectacular view of the meandering river and miles of forest to the east. Bring a camera! The trail winds downhill to the parking area at Marilla Road.

Retrace the ride to return to Coates Highway. On the return, watch for a marked fork at about 16.5 miles. Ride or walk up 200 yards to the Redhill Lookout for a panoramic view of the area to the southwest.

17 Betsie River Pathway

Type:	Loops
Distance:	8 miles
Time:	1.5 to 3 hours
Trail Type:	Mixture of singletrack and twotrack
Elevation Gain:	100 feet
Difficulty:	Easy
Location:	Benzie County - Pere Marquette State Forest
Comments:	Flat ride that can be enjoyed by everyone. The two loops offer a tremendous contrast in scenery.

Betsie River Pathway is a great ride for all skill levels. The terrain is exceptionally flat. The winding singletrack is a great place to sharpen riding skills. The river loop passes through a beautiful hardwood forest and offers views of the Betsie River. Additional riding is available on the twotracks that crisscross through the area. Camping is available to the south at Healy Lake, and to the north on the Platte River. I swam in the Betsie River. Sleeping Bear Dunes are nearby for an awe inspiring sunset and swimming in Lake Michigan.

The pathway is located off of M-115 between Cadillac and Frankfort. From Cadillac, head north on M-115. About three miles after passing the entrance to Crystal Mountain Ski Area turn left onto King Road. After 1.3 miles, turn left onto Longstreet Road. This turn was unmarked. Longstreet is the first major dirt road. The parking area is 3/4 mile ahead on the left.

Leave the trailhead via the right fork in the trail. The enjoyable ride from Point 1 to Point 2 is flat, windy, and characteristic of this loop. The turns are tight and the singletrack is in great condition. I had a blast! Pedal into

Point 2 at 1.2 miles. Here the trail is in a nice clearing with a splattering of old apple trees.

From Point 2, take the right fork and continue the flat, winding trail to Point 3. At Point 3, take the right fork again and continue on the singletrack through a young forest. After passing two twotracks, the trail turns to twotrack as it enters a stand of pines. Another twotrack is passed before rolling into Point 4.

Leave Point 4 via the right hand fork. The trail remains flat and winds through some hardwoods and a stand of pines before entering a large clearing. The trail turns into a twotrack, heading towards a stand of pines. Stay along the left edge of the clearing. At about 4.8 miles, a singletrack leaves the twotrack on the left and returns to the parking area.

To start the second loop, cross Longstreet Road. Go right at the intersection at Point 6 after passing through an old orchard. The trail crosses a couple of twotracks before reaching Point 7. After a thrilling downhill, the trail enters a beautiful, mature hardwood forest. This loop is a tremendous contrast to the loop on the other side of the road. In the spring and early summer, this area is populated with the marvelous, white, trillium wildflower.

At Point 8 there is a "Y" intersection. Both forks reach Point 9. I have always gone right to get a look at the Betsie River and go for a swim. After passing the river, the trail climbs sharply to Point 9. Take the right fork and ride the gorgeous singletrack through the hardwoods. Upon exiting the forest, the trail returns to the orchard and Point 6. Cross the road and return to the parking area.

18 Lost Lake Pathway

Type: Loops
Distance: 6.5 miles
Time: 1 to 2 hours
Trail Type: Mixture of singletrack and twotrack
Elevation Gain: Less than 100 feet
Difficulty: Family - Easy
Location: Grand Traverse County - Pere Marquette State Forest
Comments: Nearly totally flat ride that passes three lakes and a stream.

Lost Lake Pathway is a great place for beginning riders, families, or groups of mixed abilities. The trail is basically level and winds through a beautiful area just outside of Traverse City. The trail is well marked. Camping and swimming are available at Lake Dubonnet.

The ride is located southwest of Traverse City off of US-31 by Lake Dubonnet. From Traverse City, go west on US-31. Turn north on Wildwood Road and travel one mile to the parking area.

Leave the parking area via the singletrack that starts behind the information center. For the first 1/2 mile, the trail winds through the hardwoods and crosses two dirt roads. The trail then passes along the shore of Lake Dubonnet and skirts the edge of the campground. After passing a well at 1.2 miles, take a sharp left turn and ride away from the shore of the lake.

At 1.4 miles is the junction for Point 2. So far, the ride has been basically flat. Curve right onto the wide dirt road and pedal across the earthen dam. Point 3 is on the left, 20-30 yards after crossing the dam. The trail is slightly sandy and rough from horse travel as it continues along the stream that left Lake Dubonnet. The trail damage can be attributed to riders of the Shore-To-Shore equestrian trail that pass through the area.

After leaving Point 3, the trail forks at the first hill on the ride. The left fork is less sandy and an easier climb as the trail turns away from the stream. The trail remains well marked as it crosses several twotracks before rolling into Point 4.

At the junction for Point 4, go left. The trail is flat as it winds out and around Lost Lake. After crossing a twotrack, enjoy a pleasant downhill section along the edge of a marsh.

At about 3.9 miles, pedal into Point 5. After leaving Point 5, the trail merges with a wider trail and climbs the largest hill on the ride. For the next mile, the trail gently rolls before arriving at Point 6.

At Point 6, go left and ride to the familiar junction at Point 3. Ride back over the dam to Point 2. At Point 2, go right and head into the hardwoods. At the fork, 100 yards from Point 2, go left on the singletrack. The trail gradually climbs a ridge above a small lake. At the end of the lake, take the left fork as the trail splits. Continue on the singletrack, cross a dirt road, and return to the parking area.

19 Lake Ann Pathway

Type: Loop
Distance: 5 miles
Time: 1 to 2 hours
Trail Type: Singletrack
Elevation Gain: 200 feet
Difficulty: Difficult
Location: Benzie County - Pere Marquette State Forest
Comments: Tremendous hills, four lakes, and a river all packed into five miles. Plan on riding the hilly loop several times.

Don't let the shortness of this ride fool you. The loops on the west side of Reynolds Road offer one of the most challenging sets of hills in this book. Be careful. Several accidents have been reported on the steep descents. If you love lung busting and thigh burning climbs, like I do, this is a great ride. Camping and swimming are available at Lake Ann.

The Lake Ann Pathway is located west of Traverse City between M-72 and US-31. Turn on to Reynolds Road from either highway. Follow Reynolds Road to the parking area on the west side of Lake Ann.

From the parking area, go left across the dirt road on the singletrack. At Point 3, go right, and quickly come upon the shallow running Platte River. The trail drops smartly through the hardwood forest before dumping out onto the shore of the beautiful Lake Ann. The trail passes Point 4 as it continues along the shore. A sharp left leads away from the lake and past a boat launch. The trail winds behind the campground before ending up back at Point 2.

Cross Reynolds Road and immediately come upon Point 5. Go right and wind past Shavenaugh Lake. The trail starts to climb here. After dropping to the shore of Mary's Lake, the trail climbs again to Point 6.

Leave Point 6 via the right fork. After more climbing and dropping, the trail forks just prior to Point 7. Both forks are valid. At Point 7, the trail forks again. The left fork is definitely worth exploring, but leave it for later. Take the right fork and leave Point 7. Pass above another lake on the right and continue to climb and drop through the hardwood forest. The hills increase in size in this, the back section of the trail.

After passing Point 8, watch for a sharp left turn on a steep drop. The trail continues to drop before passing along the Platte River for 1/4 mile. Climb up and away from the river before rolling down to Point 9.

From the "T" intersection at Point 9, go right to continue the loop. A left turn would lead back to Point 7. After 1/2 mile of riding a ridge above the river, the trail rolls into Point 10. Point 10 is another "T" intersection. The left turn leads to Point 6. I rode in this direction since I went around the loop several more times.

To return to the parking area from Point 6, go right and climb a slightly sandy hill. Roll down to Point 5. Go right and re-cross Reynolds Road.

20 Vasa Pathway

Type: Loop
Distance: 15.5 miles
Time: 2 to 5 hours
Trail Type: Twotrack
Elevation Gain: 1000 feet
Difficulty: Difficult
Location: Pere Marquette State Forest
Comments: A wonderful ride offering several challenging climbs.

The Vasa Pathway is home to the Ice Man Cometh mountain bike race and the Vasa X-C ski race. Set entirely on twotracks, the ride includes some huge climbs and long, fast descents. The ride is sandy in spots. Seek out some firmer riding area along the edge of the twotrack to save strength for the climbs. Twotracks and singletracks too numerous to mention cut through the ride. Allow time to do some exploring. The trail is well marked with distance markers in kilometers. Camping and swimming are abundant in the area.

The pathway is located southeast of Traverse City. Head east on M-72 to Bunker Hill Road. Turn right on Bunker Hill and drive one mile to Barret Road. Go right. The parking area is 3/4 mile up on the left.

From the large parking area, leave on the wood chip covered twotrack. Cross Acme Creek at the 1 Km mark. The next several kilometers climb steadily. At 2 Kms, the trail drops sharply down into a sandy fork. Go left and continue into the mixed pine and oak forest.

The terrain rolls to a major fork just short of the 4 Km mark. Go left for the 25 Km loop. After passing the 5 Km mark on a nice downhill, the twotrack turns sandy. Watch for better riding areas along the edge of the twotrack, particularly when climbing.

The twotrack climbs gradually to a marked "Y" intersection just past 7 Kms. The right fork leads back to the 10 Km loop for a total of 13 Km. Go left. The trail has climbed a little less than 400 feet to this point.

On an improved surface, enjoy a long, fast descent before climbing two short hills to reach the 8 Km mark. The twotrack climbs steadily before reaching the big climb of the ride. The hill is sandy, steep, long, and had me sweating. Watch for a particularly sandy stretch halfway up that took away my momentum. Don't stop to pant at the summit! Ride down the long, sweet, refreshing descents that occur until the 10 Km mark.

Climbing, the twotrack enters, then exits a hardwood forest. The trail crosses a small meadow. Veer right and exit the meadow via the righthand corner. After a short sandy section, the twotrack is covered with gravel and riding improved. The next several kilometers are flat.

Just prior to the 14 Km mark, go left onto the "expert" terrain. The next 2 Kms are grassy and somewhat rough with some good climbs as the terrain starts to roll.

Around the 16 Km mark, the twotrack flattens and turns sandy in spots. This continues as the twotrack passes under powerlines and into a clear-cut area. The riding improves while passing through another stand of hardwoods. The twotrack rolls gradually until the 21 Km mark.

In general, the rest of the trail is downhill. Enjoy some long descents interrupted by short climbs. Be aware that once the trail is covered with wood chips again, traffic is two-way.

21 Sand Lakes Quiet Area

Type:	Loop
Distance:	8 miles with possibilities for much more
Time:	1 to 3 hours
Trail Type:	Mixture of singletrack and twotrack
Elevation Gain:	200 feet
Difficulty:	Moderate
Location:	Grand Traverse County - Pere Marquette State Forest
Comments:	Truly an outstanding ride with a tremendous amount of variety.

The Sand Lakes ride was, without exception, the first ride mentioned by the all the Traverse City riders I questioned. High praise, and well deserved. The ride has several challenging climbs and thrilling descents. There are even some tight, hair-pin turns similar to Yankee Springs. For more riding, try exploring the twotracks in the area. I was in the mood for a longer ride so I made a loop, on twotracks, from Kalkaska. Any fishermen should strap a pole on their top bar. The trail can access more than a dozen lakes and the North Branch of the Bordman River. Camping and swimming are available at Guernsey Lake State Forest Campground.

The main trailhead for the ride is located between Kalkaska and Traverse City, south of M-72. From M-72, turn south onto Broomhead Road. The trailhead is on the left after about four miles.

A wide, flat trail leaves from the information center at the south end of the parking area. Get ready as the trail drops for nearly a mile on the way to Point 2. Watch for some tight, slalom-like turns during the descent. Roll past Point 2 and continue the gradual downhill to Point 3.

At Point 3, turn left, and pedal the short distance to Point 5. To the right of Point 5 is a picnic table, well, and Lake 1. The lake looks like a great place for a swim. If time permits, bring a picnic lunch to take advantage of these conveniences. Point 5 is a fork. The left fork is a twotrack for exploring. Continue via the right fork on the great singletrack. The trail starts to roll on the way to Point 6.

Point 6 is another fork. The right fork leads to Point 7 and accesses Lake 2, Lake 4 and Lake 5. Plan on checking it out. The inner portion of the loop contains some great terrain. I rode left, and a stone's throw away passed the junction for Point 8. The left fork at Point 8 is a twotrack that leads to Roots Lakes. Go right. On the way to Point 9, the trail continues to roll through the forest and skirts the shore of a drying-up lake.

A twotrack intersects the trail at Point 9. Continue straight. The next section of trail is fantastic. After narrowing to a singletrack, the trail gradually rolls, and passes through a set of challenging, short, sharp turns. Pedal into Point 10. Go right on the wide flat twotrack. Roll past the next junction, which is Point 11, and continue on to Point 12.

Point 12 is the junction of three trails. Over my left shoulder was an inviting trail I did not explore. To my left was a trail that went up a hill and passed the campground on the way to the river. If time permits, check both of these trails out. To continue to Point 13, go right. The trail is wide, and slightly uphill as it rolls past a marsh, through Point 13, and into Point 14. At Point 13, check out the rugged, downhill trail that bisects the twotrack. This is a tough climb on a steep hill with several tree roots crossing the trail. Try to work this portion of the trail in as a downhill section.

At Point 14 the trail merges with an equestrian trail. Continue straight around the gate to check out the river. Go right and prepare for a great section of snaking, little turns. The turns are 30-40 yards apart and some are nicely banked. I was flying through this section, taking advantage of the slight drop in the trail. Fantastic riding! This section ends all too quickly as it emerges from the thick stand of trees. Make a sharp right and endure a sandy trail for a short distance. At the crest of the hill, the trail improves and arrives at Point 15. Go left. The trail climbs, and is slightly sandy most of the 3/4 mile to Point 16.

Point 16 is another "Y" intersection. The area near the junction is populated with dogwoods that spectacularly flower in the late spring. Both forks offer great riding. Pick a direction and eventually climb to Point 18. From Point 18, pedal up the steep hill past Point 2 and back to the parking area.

22 Schuss Mountain

Type:	Loop
Distance:	5.5
Time:	30 to 90 minutes
Trail Type:	Mixture of singletrack and twotrack
Elevation Gain:	783 feet
Difficulty:	Difficult
Location:	Antrim County
Comments:	Site of the 1993 NORBA national cross country mountain bike race. A navigational challenge.

Schuss Mountain and Shanty Creek Resort were the site of the 1993 NORBA nationals. The trail described is the race course for the cross country event. The professional racers went around five times. After riding the trail a number of times you will find that all the turns and intersections make this a marvelous ride. The first couple of rides may be a little frustrating for the same reason. Camping and swimming are abundant close by.

The trail is located at Schuss Mountain Resort, west of Mancelona. From M-88, follow the signs to the resort. Once in the resort area, follow the signs to the hotel at the base of the ski hill.

The trail starts next to the "black" chairlift, to the right of the hotel. This course was newly designed for the nationals. The trail utilizes some X-C ski trails and twotracks. I was lucky enough to ride the course the day after a shake-out race so I found it well marked. If it was not marked, I probably would not have made all the right turns to follow the race course.

The trail starts climbing on a twotrack. Some major

construction was occurring along the first couple of hundred
yards of the trail. Stay to the left on the twotrack. Several
other twotracks will intersect in the first couple of hundred
yards. The twotrack ends abruptly and a tight, twisty,
technical singletrack climbs to the Chickens Choice downhill
ski run at .3 miles. Go right and climb on Chickens Choice to
Mellow Yellow ski run. Go right on the twotrack and continue
to climb. At the junction of the Hilltop Loop ski run, go right.

At 1.3 miles make a sharp left. At 1.4 miles go right at the
"Y" intersection. At 1.5 miles, go sharply left just before
reaching a sandy twotrack. At 1.8 miles, the wide singletrack
crosses the twotrack and continues in the hardwoods. The trail
parallels the twotrack before merging onto it for a short
distance. At the fork, go left for 20 yards, then veer right onto
a singletrack that is passing through a meadow. At the edge of
the meadow, follow the twotrack leaving on the right. The two
mile point was passed in the meadow.

Leaving the meadow, the twotrack rolls through a fantastic
section of quick rolling hills - roller coaster ride. Each hill is
30 to 50 feet of gain and drop. There must have been seven or
eight hills, but I was having too much fun to count.

At 2.4 miles, go left at the "Y" intersection. Go left at the
second "Y" and climb a gradual hill. At 2.6 miles, take the
singletrack on the left. The trail continues to climb through
the hardwoods before reaching a large meadow. Go sharply
left. The trail continues along the left edge of the meadow
before veering right on the twotrack. At about three miles, the
twotrack has crossed the meadow and reentered the hardwoods.
The last mile climbed nearly the whole way.

The twotrack drops splendidly in the hardwoods before taking a sharp right to cross a dirt road. The turn comes while still descending on the hill, so watch for it. After crossing the dirt road, the trail turns to singletrack. At the next "T" intersection, go left onto the twotrack. The twotrack rolls downhill to another "T". Go right. Fly downhill on the twotrack. At 3.6 miles, veer right onto a singletrack just as the twotrack bends left. The trail winds through a sparsely forested meadow. At about four miles, the trail reenters the hardwoods.

After reentering the hardwoods, the next 1/2 mile of riding is fantastic. The singletrack is tight, twisting, and turning with a number of short undulations. No big climbs. Major emphasis on bike handling skills.

At 4.5 miles the singletrack merges into a twotrack. Climb uphill on the twotrack. At the crest of the hill, go right onto a singletrack which dumps onto a downhill ski run after about 20 yards. It appeared that the trail was designed to meander back and forth across the sandy ski run. Pick the best line down the hill to pick up a trail on the right that goes into the hardwoods.

Once in the hardwoods, fly down the singletrack. Go left at the fork and continue downhill. Go left at the next "T" intersection. The trail is now just about back at the hotel and the outdoor pool looked inviting. The trail started to the left, by the black chairlift. Remember, the racers went around five times!

23 Jordan River Pathway

Type:	Loop
Distance:	17 miles
Time:	3 to 6 hours
Trail Type:	Singletrack and one mile of twotrack
Elevation Gain:	1300 feet
Difficulty:	Difficult
Log Crossings:	373 (approximate)
Location:	Atrium County - Mackinaw State Forest
Comments:	Easily the most technical and physically demanding ride in the book. Advanced riders will either love or hate this ride.

This ride travels through the magnificent Jordan River Valley. The technical aspect of the ride comes from heavily eroded trails, low bridges (logs/trees crossing the trail that may be too low to ride under), steep climbs and descents, long sections of riding through damp areas with heavy concentrations of exposed tree roots, numerous narrow "bridges", and hundreds of logs to jump or carry a bike over. If you read the above list as negatives, it is probably best to pick another ride. Personally, I think it is fantastic to have a technical ride like this one in the state. Anyone planning on riding some of the more difficult rides in the west should practice on this ride. This is the only ride I found in Michigan that offers anything like the trails in Colorado, Wyoming, Utah and Idaho. Camping is available on the trail or at the Graves Crossing Campground at the west end of the trail.

The pathway is located on Deadmans Hill Road, six miles north of Mancelona, off of US-131. Before starting the ride, walk up to the view area on Deadmans Hill to get a perspective of the ride. In the fall this area is bursting with color.

Get settled and clipped in at the trailhead because the trail starts with a grand descent where the slightest release of the brake lever results in a surge of acceleration and adrenaline. The trail drops at least 300 feet on the descent. As is the case with all the descents on the trail, be prepared to encounter a log or two at maximum speed! A sharp, sandy turn marks Point 3.

Leaving Point 3, the next 1/2 mile is a sampler of several other sections of the trail. The singletrack is heavily eroded in spots, covered with logs, and sidecut into the hill. The trail forks at about the one mile mark. Go left to return to the parking area. Go right to continue.

The sound of bullfrogs singing told me I was coming into a stretch of wetlands before I saw the old beaver ponds on both sides of the trail. The trail is riding on an old railroad grade, so is dry and flat. Indian paintbrushes and daisies are abundant through this section of the trail.

The trail is flat or slightly downhill until reaching Marsh Road. Go right and use the road to cross the shallow, quick running Jordan River. I paused on the bridge long enough to spot some small brook trout fighting the strong current in an eddy. The trail stays on the road for .1 mile before leaving on the left.

The "quality" of the trail degrades (or improves) as it nears the river's edge. Tree roots fill the eroded, damp trail. The beautiful Jordan River is unlike any other river in the book. The course of the river is redirected around hundreds of "islands" of downed trees. Soil has accumulated on the decaying trees and the islands support trees, grasses, and wildflowers. Truly unique and beautiful.

The trail continues to challenge the rider before reaching Point 10. A few hills, lots of logs, some tree roots, and a few wet spots are passed as the trail travels along and above the river. Somewhere in this section I sunk in mud up to my front hub, rendering my computer useless until I noticed it sometime later. In this section I was lucky enough to spy a beaver waddling to the safety of the river. My first out-of-water sighting! Watch for the abundant beaver signs along the trail.

Leaving Point 10, the trail is flat and fast as it travels along on another old railroad grade. Get into that big chainring and take advantage of the relatively unobstructed riding. The trail leaves the railroad grade to the right and climbs steadily, and at times, steeply, up a ridge. This is the first real climb of the ride. The winding trail passes through the maple forest on top of the ridge before entering a clearing. Take some time to stop and enjoy the incredible view from atop the ridge.

Leaving the clearing, the trail descends spectacularly before entering the Pinney Bridge Campground. There is a well in the campground. Turn right and keep the information center on the right to reach a twotrack, 150 yards past the information center. Go left on the twotrack and drop to the river. From the view area to the river crossing, the trail drops 200 feet.

The trail crosses the river via a blocked off bridge and continues straight up the sandy twotrack. The river around the bridge is still populated with the small islands that disrupt its flow.

The sandy twotrack climbs and turns into singletrack which continues to climb the ridge. A nice grunt! Up on the top of the ridge the trail becomes exhilarating. Sudden technical drops, low bridges, technical climbs, winding flat sections through hardwoods, and lots of logs to jump contribute to a classic section of riding.

After crossing Cascade Road, the trail drops to the noisy Landslide Creek. The creek is crossed via the remains of a split log bridge. I opted to walk across the bridge once I spotted the gaps in the logs that were large enough to trap a wheel. The volume of water that feeds into the Jordan River in the next six miles is impressive. Several creeks and drainages are crossed using the split log style bridges. Be wary of the large gaps in these bridges.

After crossing the creek, the trail is covered by exposed tree roots, is eroded, and includes a steep technical climb up old, decaying steps. Truly a technical challenge. The rolling singletrack is a technical rider's dream as it continues to cross tree roots, logs, muddy areas, and water. Stopping to take a note, I enjoyed a second "wildlife" experience. A timid, white spotted fawn, no more than 18 inches tall popped out of the ferns two feet from where I had stopped. I waited long enough for the fawn to walk well away from the trail before continuing so as not to spook it again.

After crossing the second major creek, watch for a sharp left and a gonzo descent down a sandy, heavily eroded pitch. The drop includes several tight, tree lined turns. A great treat! After a long, marginally rideable section of wet, tree root covered trail next to the third fork of Landslide Creek, the trail climbs steeply in a granny gear grunt to Point 18. The marker is high on a ridge and offers another panoramic view of the Jordan River Valley.

From the overlook, take the left fork as it winds and drops to the wide, clear Section 3 Creek. After crossing the creek, the trail is firm, dry and rolling all the way to Point 20. This section of trail climbed steadily and included a high number of log crossings.

The trail continues to climb all the way to Point 23, attempting to make up the big drop in the first 1/2 mile of the trail. Glasses of some sort might be a good idea as the trail passes through a long section of spruce trees that have grown close to the trail. In several places the tree boughs cannot be avoided. I used a forearm across my face, which was marginally effective.

Leaving the spruce planting, the trail is fast, winding, and almost clear of logs the remainder of the ride. A great section of riding, but uncharacteristic for the rest of the trail. Let out some frustration and crank away. After passing Point 23, the trail merges back with a three mile loop that is popular with hikers. Practice courteous riding habits here and share the trail so that the ride will stay open to mountain bikes.

The trail eventually ends at a sandy dirt road. Go right, then immediately left to return to the trailhead.

24 Wildwood Hills Pathway

Type:	Loop
Distance:	9.5 miles
Time:	1 to 2 hours
Trail Type:	Twotrack
Elevation Gain:	600 feet
Difficulty:	Moderate
Location:	Cheboygan County - Mackinaw State Forest
Comments:	A classic set of Michigan twotrack that gradually climbs and drops through the entire ride.

Riders who enjoy cruising twotracks will love this ride. The trail has everything a great twotrack ride should have: recent and ancient logging activity, large stands of hardwoods and pines, old buildings, lots of crisscrossing twotracks to explore, and large meadows of tall grasses and wildflowers. Camping and swimming are located at Blurt Lake State Park, about six miles north.

The ride itself is well marked, but the typical (and helpful) DNR Pathway signs that direct you to the trailhead are missing. Take Old 27 to Wildwood Road, which is about halfway between Wolverine and Indian River. Turn west onto Wildwood Road. The parking area for the ride is about three miles from Old 27.

The trail starts at Point 4 in the DNR numbering scheme. This is the east parking area for the ride. Take the twotrack to the right of the trailhead. After 100 yards, turn right onto the first twotrack that intersects the trail. After about 1/2 mile, Point 3 is reached. Go left at the fork at Point 3.

The twotrack climbs steadily then drops to a "T" intersection at

1.7 miles. Go sharply right. The twotrack climbs and drops through pines and then maples before veering right at a "T" intersection at 2.2 miles.

After passing a few of the informational signs that mark past logging activity in the area, enjoy a long gradual downhill to reach Point 6. Negotiate the sandy intersection and make a sharp left turn. Leaving Point 6, enjoy a couple of more long downhills before reaching a blind right turn at 3.4 miles. The ferns had grown so high I never saw the twotrack until I was past it.

At 3.6 miles, Point 7 is reached. Cross Ream Road. About 3/4 mile after leaving Point 7, a "T" intersection is encountered. Go right. The left fork leads to the abandoned Lost Tamarack Pathway. This trail is about 1.5 miles away and is approximately nine miles, round-trip.

After passing through a large field, Point 8 is reached just before crossing a sandy twotrack. Go left across the twotrack to include a singletrack that climbs and then descends about 40 feet. This spur trail merges back with the main trail after a short distance. At 5.5 miles, another spur trail crosses the dirt road the trail has been paralleling since leaving Point 8. The spur trail includes 100 feet of climbing and a long gradual drop of the same amount.

Just before reaching Point 9, a short singletrack section merges into a maple tree shaded twotrack. The twotrack is the remains of a turn of the century railroad grade used to transport lumber to neighboring mills. The twotrack is slightly downhill and clear, making for a great chance to get into the upper chainring and cruise all the way to Point 1.

The twotrack leaving Point 1 was supposed to include a couple of spur trails with more climbing. I missed these intersections while admiring the large meadows filled with wildflowers. After crossing Ream Road again, go right at the first "Y" intersection.

Go left leaving Point 2. Enjoy a short climb and then a long gradual downhill that will carry you to Point 3. Go left at Point 3 and return to the parking area.

25 Ocqueoc Falls Bicentennial Pathway

Type:	Loops
Distance:	3 or 6 miles
Time:	1 hour
Trail Type:	Twotrack
Elevation Gain:	200 feet
Difficulty:	Family - Easy
Location:	Presque Isle County - Mackinaw State Forest
Comments:	This ride starts from the largest falls in the Lower Peninsula. The ride passes along the river and through the surrounding forest.

A scenic twotrack cruise that finishes at the largest natural whirlpool in the Lower Peninsula. Be sure to bring a swimsuit to enjoy the warm water in the natural pool created by the six foot waterfall. The whitewater in the river is warmer than any of the lakes this far north. The ride is generally flat, but includes a few surprising drops and dips. All the climbs are easily managed or pushed. Beginners should limit themselves to the three mile loop. The campground at the falls was closed in July of 1993. Camping is also available on Lake Huron and Black Lake.

The trail is located 11 miles west of Rogers City, just off of M-68. The trail starts from the parking area for the falls.

From the information center, go right into a stand of surreal looking red pines. The flat twotrack passes through the pines which give way to beeches which change to birches and aspens before returning to pines. At 1.5 miles, Point 2 is reached. The trail has been dry, firm, and covered by pine needles. Go left for the three mile loop. Go right to complete the longer loop. At 1.8 miles, a caution sign warns of a sandy drop to the rusty colored Little Ocqueoc River.

Leaving the river, the twotrack climbs just a little to reach Point 3. The intersection is found just after riding through a beautiful field covered with wildflowers. Go left to reach the river and shorten the ride.

After about three miles, the trail starts to bend left in a large meadow. This starts the return segment of the ride. After a couple of good drops, the trail enters an area with some obvious signs of camping activity. The river is on the right, about 75 feet below the trail. The trail follows the twotrack along the river after leaving the camping area. After a short plunge of about 30 feet, Point 4 is passed. At 4.2 miles, the trail drops to cross the Little Ocqueoc River again. Leaving the river, the trail rolls gradually.

After about five miles, the trail drops right to the edge of the river. The remainder of the ride keeps the river in view. Watch for several one foot deep depressions on the trail. The trail ends at the falls. Go get the swimsuit and enjoy the natural whirlpool. If you can move some of the locals out of the way, you can stand right under the falls and use the water to relax some of those sore muscles.

26 Shingle Mill Pathway

Type:	Loops
Distance:	6, 10, or 11 miles
Time:	1 to 3 hours
Trail Type:	Mixture of singletrack and twotrack
Elevation Gain:	300 feet
Difficulty:	Moderate
Location:	Otsego and Cheboygan Counties - Pigeon River State Forest
Comments:	Predominately flat ride through the rugged, wild, and scenic Pigeon River country.

The Shingle Mill Pathway is a DNR constructed loop on the High Country Pathway. The ride includes long stretches of flat singletrack, views of the Pigeon River, and panoramic views of the area. Much of the trail passes through a mixed pine forest which thrives in the slightly sandy soils. Camping and swimming are available at the trailhead.

The pathway starts at the Pigeon River Bridge Campground, eleven miles east of Vanderbilt. Park in the large area across the street from the campground and the trailhead.

Take the wide singletrack from the trailhead and pedal through the pine and beech forest past Point 2 and Point 3. Leaving Point 3, the trail travels along the river for too short of a distance before continuing on a ridge above the beaver created wetlands.

After about two miles, the Pigeon River forest area headquarters are encountered. To find out more about the area, stop in the office and purchase the "Field Guide to the High Country Pathway." An excellent informational pamphlet describing the area. Buildings that house the rangers were originally constructed by the Civilian Conservation Corps in the 1930's.

The terrain rolls slightly with some long, pleasant downhills before reaching the Pigeon River Campground at 2.75 miles. The trail passes though the campground on the campground roads. At three miles, cross the river via a bridge. The singletrack trail restarts immediately across the bridge on the right.

After riding the ridge above the river, the trail reaches Point 6. Go left at this intersection for the six mile loop. The right fork leads to the longer loops. The trail to Point 7 is a great stretch of singletrack. The trail twists and turns on a high ridge above the river.

Point 7 is a fork. I went right for the 11 mile loop. This segment of trail was damp in spots and included some rugged riding through a bog with the deep rich smell of decaying wood. The segment passes an old logging campsite and a beaver dam as well. The left fork shortens the ride to 10 miles. This segment of trail passes a "sinkhole" lake and continues along the shore of Grass Lake. Both forks climb through hardwoods before reuniting at Point 10.

At Point 10, take the left spur to the Grass Lake Overlook. The overlook is a great place to snack or lunch and enjoy the truly magnificent view of Grass Lake and the Pigeon River valley.

Leaving Point 10, the trail continues through the hardwoods to Point 11. The High Country Pathway leaves the Shingle Mill Pathway at this intersection. Go left. The trail drops steadily off the hardwood covered hill, past a small lake, and back into the river valley. Once in the river valley, the trail is flat again as it passes Grass Lake and Ford Lake.

Shortly after skirting the shore of Ford Lake, Point 12 is reached. I rode straight, or south. This segment of trail passes through a cedar swamp on the longest stretch of corduroy bridge I have ever seen. The out-of-saddle riding is rough and the bridge was slippery. Common sense told me to walk long stretches rather than attempt to ride. Exiting the 1/3 mile swamp, the trail improves and passes along the river before returning to the parking area.

An alternative to the swamp and the bridge would be to go left at Point 12. This would lead to Point 6 on the river and return to the trailhead via the excellent, firm, singletrack on the east side of the river.

27 Chippewa Hills Pathway

Type:	Loop
Distance:	6.5 miles
Time:	1 hour
Trail Type:	Singletrack
Elevation Gain:	450 feet
Difficulty:	Moderate
Location:	Alpena County - Mackinaw State Forest
Comments:	A fast, firm singletrack flier. My favorite ride in this quadrant of the state.

Chippewa Hills Pathway was a great break for me from the flat, wet rides that I had found in the northeast side of the state. After the initial descent of about 100 feet, I knew I was going to enjoy this singletrack. The trail rolls through the hardwood and aspen covered hills. No big climbs are included, making this a great destination ride for a group or club of regular riders. If you liked Cadillac Pathway or Sand Lakes Quiet Area, you will enjoy this ride as well. Camping and swimming can be found on the shore of Lake Huron.

The ride is located northwest of the north end of Hubbard Lake. From US-23, turn west on Nicholson Road. After about 11 miles, turn south on Kissau Road to reach the parking area.

Leave the information center via the right fork to reach Point 1. Get clipped in at the trailhead because the trail drops almost 100 feet before starting to roll. At .6 miles, Point 2 is passed. The singletrack drops another 50 feet after leaving Point 2. Point 3 is reached after a series of short climbs.

Leaving Point 3, the trail includes at least six exciting drops and climbs. My speed from the drops carried me nearly to the crest of the next rise. A fantastic section of riding! The drops were a little rough and sandy at the base, adding to the excitement.

The trail drops beautifully through the hardwoods to cross a small creek via a new bridge. Go around a gate and climb a twotrack to reach Point 5 at 2.4 miles. Watch for small triangular signs with exclamation points that mark some of the bigger drops on the ride.

The singletrack leaves Point 5 and climbs steadily to Point 6. A long, gradual descent is found after the climb to Point 6. This drop is followed by another long gradual climb. Great section of riding! Point 7 is passed after dropping to cross a small, rough twotrack.

The small loop east of the twotrack just crossed climbs through a beautiful stand of tall aspens. The aspens give way to the thick pines just before recrossing the twotrack. The remainder of the trail, about three miles, is a wonderful stretch of singletrack. The trail rolls, but steadily climbs to regain all the elevation lost in the first mile of riding. Too soon, the trail returns to the parking area. I had so much fun that I went around two more times and fell in love with this ride.

28   Hartwick Pines State Park

Type:	Loops
Distance:	7.5, 5, and 3 miles
Time:	30 to 90 minutes
Trail Type:	Twotrack
Elevation Gain:	300 feet
Difficulty:	Family - Moderate
Location:	Crawford County
Comments:	A relatively easy twotrack ride that includes a number of exciting downhills on the backstretch. An advanced family ride due to the hills.

Hartwick Pines State Park was created to preserve one of the last stands of virgin white pine in the state. A wonderful interpretive hike includes a lumbering museum, several restored Civilian Conservation Corps buildings, and the majestic pines. The trail is an unimaginative rectangle that is segmented into three distances. The last stretch of riding includes a number of thrilling drops and a couple of short climbs. Camping is available in the park.

The park is located northeast of Grayling on M-93. Park in the Pines Picnic Area.

Construction of a road was occurring when I rode the trail so things may change for the start of the ride. From the parking area, ride to the paved road that forked to the right, immediately after the admission gate. The trail starts on the right, about 50 yards from the start of the paved fork.

The trail is totally flat, passing through a pine forest before reaching Point 1. At 1.7 miles, go left at the intersection to ride the three mile loop. Point 2 is reached at about 2.4 miles.

Go left at Point 2 to eliminate some hills and distance. The left fork is for the five mile loop.

Leaving Point 2, the twotrack starts to climb and roll as it enters a beautiful stand of hardwoods. The fallen leaf covered trail turns left at Point 3. After passing Point 3, the shady twotrack meanders wonderfully through the tall hardwoods. The whine of I-75 is persistent in the background.

The trail turns sharply left upon reaching some powerlines. Enjoy three to four thrilling drops before passing Point 4. The drops are a little rough but easily rideable. This segment of trail also includes one good climb that may need to be pushed by beginning riders.

The trail continues to drop and roll under the old powerlines before reaching a paved road. If the hills have taken their toll, go right on the paved road to return to the parking area. The twotrack climbs and reenters the white pines after crossing the paved road.

Point 5 is passed at 6.5 miles. At 6.8 miles, a warning sign proceeds a thrilling plunge that includes a sharp right hand turn. The twotrack crosses a dirt road and passes part of the interpretive trail at the base of this hill. Enjoy one last short climb after crossing the dirt road. A big drop from the last ascent brings the trail to a paved road, where the trail ends. Go right and pedal the short distance to the parking area.

29 Wakely Lake

Type:	Loop
Distance:	4 to 22 miles
Time:	1 hour to all day
Trail Type:	Twotrack
Elevation Gain:	0 feet
Difficulty:	Family - Easy
Location:	Crawford County - Huron National Forest
Comments:	The best family ride I found. A ride to go slow, stop often, and absorb the beauty of the area.

Wakely Lake Non-Motorized Area has been set aside as a nesting site for the common loon and the bald eagle. The area is gorgeous. The terrain is flat and the trails are firm and dry. A four mile marked loop circles the beautiful lake and nearby wetlands. Only a few small hills are climbed. The downhills are gradual and the trail is wide, making this a great ride for less experienced riders. The area is crisscrossed by grassy twotracks, making this a great area for exploring. Bird watchers and fishermen will enjoy this area. Bird watchers have spotted over 115 different bird species in the area. The ranger told me the lake is the home for record sized pan-fish (the lake was catch and release in 1993). Combine this ride with the Mason Tract trail a couple of miles away for a great weekend of riding and camping. Camping is available at several places on the Au Sable River and Kneff Lake. Kneff Lake also has a nice, sandy swimming area.

The trail is located about 10 miles east of Grayling on M-72. The parking area is on the north side of the road.

From the parking area, ride on the twotrack for 100 yards before picking up a singletrack leaving to the left. This trail glides downhill to the shore of Wakely Lake. Eventually the trail passes between the lake and a water lily covered pond. At 1.4 miles, go right at the fork, following the blue blazes on the trees. The riding from the lake to the intersection rolls through a series of hills that are 10 to 15 feet high. The trail turns often, but is well marked, as a series of twotracks crisscross through the area. At 2.3 miles, go right at the "T" intersection for the family ride. The left option leads to slightly more rolling terrain and accesses the farthest reaches of the area. The riding on the left fork is well worth exploring.

As the trail passes over the origin of Wakely Creek, watch for a well defined trail crossing the narrow earthen dam. The trail was created by tail dragging beavers crossing between the lake and the creek. Shortly after crossing the small dam, the trail passes a dike that was built to enhance the nesting area for the loons. The dikes are closed to bikes at all times and to everyone during nesting season.

A four way intersection marks the three mile point of the ride. Go right for the four mile loop. The trail rolls gradually downhill to a beautiful, pine shaded camping and picnic area on the shore of the lake. From this point, it is only one mile, round-trip, to the parking area to get lunch, fishing gear, the binoculars, and the camera.

The remainder of the area offers great riding. Don't attempt to follow some of the marked trails. Most proved to be too rough to ride. Instead, cruise the area on the plentiful twotracks. I rode 22 miles the morning I was in the area.

30 Mason Tract Pathway

Type: Out and Back
Distance: 11.5 miles
Time: 1 to 3 hours
Trail Type: Singletrack
Elevation Gain: 100 feet
Difficulty: Family - Easy
Location: Crawford County - Au Sable State Forest
Comments: A splendid ride along the gorgeous Au Sable River for families, fishermen, or fanatics about flat riding.

Skirting the edge of the South Branch of the Au Sable River, the Mason Tract Pathway offers a unique opportunity to enjoy this beautiful river on a mountain bike. The river is either visible or a short distance away from the trail for 80% of the ride. Fishermen should strap a rod to their top bar and try landing a trout. The ride is basically flat and well marked, making for easy riding. Pack a lunch and plan on spending the day. A campground is located on the trail.

The trail is located 15 miles east of Grayling on M-72. The parking area is on the south side of M-72, on Chase Bridge Road.

The trail starts in a dry area, sparsely populated with Jack Pines. Pedal on the flat singletrack past Point 2. Several trails intersect the main trail while riding through the campground area. Stay on the well marked, main trail. The first view of the river is available upon reaching Point 3.

At Point 3, the trail forks. Go right. On the return trip consider taking the left fork, which passes between the river and the campground. The trail climbs a ridge above the river

before offering a long, gradual downhill that carried me all the
way to Point 4. Be ready for some unexpected depressions in
the trail while rolling downhill.

The "steep" climb on the ride is between Point 4 and Point 5
at about two miles. Point 5 is in a lush, grassy meadow that
slopes gently to the river. A great place to picnic. Contrast the
vegetation and trees in this meadow with the vegetation at the
start of the trail.

Leaving Point 5, the trail turns left and enters an area of sparse
pines just before reaching a small parking area for fishermen.
Around 2.9 miles, the trail has been rerouted to avoid a steep
depression. Veer right, away from the more defined trail and
ride on a grassy track around the depression.

Point 6 is at 3.2 miles and is shaded by huge beech trees.
Here the trail forks. Take one fork now and the other on the
return trip. Both forks reunite at Point 8. The trail crosses the
Thayer Creek before arriving at Point 8. Again the vegetation
has changed.

Pedal for 1/2 mile before reaching the river again. More
splendid views and fishing holes are passed while rolling past
Point 9 and Point 10. Point 11 is located at the intersection of
the trail and Chase Bridge Road.

Enjoy a totally different view of the river after turning around
and retracing the ride. Remember to take the two options
mentioned earlier.

31 North Higgins Lake State Park

Type:	Loops
Distance:	6.5 miles
Time:	1 to 2 hours
Trail Type:	Twotrack
Elevation Gain:	200 feet
Difficulty:	Family - Easy
Location:	Roscommon County
Comments:	A fantastic family ride. The trail includes a Civilian Conservation Corps museum and an interpretive trail.

Big sweeping turns characterize this ride on the north end of the massive Higgins Lake. The trail starts at the Civilian Conservation Corps (CCC) Museum. About a third of the ride passes a number of interpretive markers and informational signs. I learned a lot. The trail is sandy but firm and is a better choice than the South Higgins Lake ride after a rain. The unobstructed trail is exceptionally well marked. Camping and swimming are available in the park.

The park is located on the northwest end of Higgins Lake. The trail starts from the parking area for the CCC Museum.

The trail starts along a row of pine trees that separate the parking lot from a CCC field. Entering the mixed pine and hardwood forest, the trail is wide as it passes a number of interpretive stations. A fitness course also has been established along this section of the trail.

The trail climbs about 70 feet before reaching Point 2. Leaving Point 2, the trail drops gradually for 1/2 mile. This section includes several fun, wide, sweeping turns on the twotrack. At 1.3 miles, the trail nears a stand of large pines before a wide, horseshoe shaped turn changes the direction of travel.

After passing Point 3, the flat twotrack winds wonderfully through the mixed pine and hardwood forest. The trail is sandy, but covered with pine needles to provide a smooth, firm riding surface.

On the way to Point 5, watch for an old white pine and an old red pine. Both trees are marked by informational signs. Point 5 is reached at about 3.6 miles. The right fork at Point 5 is a shortcut trail. However, this fork will involve some additional climbing.

Leaving Point 5 via the left fork, the trail passes through a beautiful stand of pines. More wide, sweeping turns are found on this segment of the trail. Turns are even found in the stand of pines, which is truly uncharacteristic. Usually, trails through row-planted pines are straight, as the trail is cut between two rows of the pines.

The trail continues a slight uphill grade as the interpretive area is reentered. At about five miles the trail drops nicely. Don't slow down as the trail passes Point 7 and Point 8. Leaving Point 8, the trail climbs to a "T" intersection at Point 9. Go left.

Leaving Point 9, the trail passes a number of interpretive signs as it drops quickly into the CCC camp. The trail goes left as it enters the CCC field where the ride started. I was going too fast to make the turn so I rode through the field and back to the parking area.

32   South Higgins Lake State Park

Type: Loop
Distance: 5 miles
Time: 30 minutes to 2 hours
Trail Type: Mixture of singletrack and twotrack
Elevation Gain: Less than 100 feet
Difficulty: Family - Easy
Location: Roscommon County
Comments: A great flat ride along Marl Lake.

South Higgins Lake State Park offers some of the most popular camping and boating spots in the state. The ride along Marl Lake is a great way to combine biking with camping, boating, and swimming. The trail is totally flat and winds through a mixed hardwood and pine forest. The riding is a little rough in spots, so be prepared. The shallow water at the Higgins Lake beach is a great place for anyone to learn to swim.

The park is located at the southeast corner of Higgins Lake. The trailhead is at the Marl Lake boat launch area.

Leave the information center and follow the trail along the shore of the lake. Several fishing opportunities exist in the next two miles. A set of three bridges at 1/3 mile allow the trail to stay dry through a small bog. At 1/2 mile, the fork for a two mile loop goes right. Veer left.

The trail for the next mile can be wet for days after a strong storm. Watch for bypass trails around the muddy spots. The trail is also crossed by several roots from pine trees. The riding is a little rough.

The next fork in the trail is at Point 3. Go right for a 3.5 mile loop. At Point 4, the trail forks again. The left fork leads to the Cut River, another fishing spot. Leave Point 4 via the right, on a moss covered trail.

About 1/2 mile after leaving Point 4, the trail is covered by pine needles. It felt to me that the trail was slightly downhill until a sharp right turn at Point 7. Leaving Point 7, the trail passes close to the road that accesses the park. This segment of the trail passes through a thick hardwood forest before ending in the parking area for the boat launch.

33 Rifle River Recreation Area

Type:	Loops
Distance:	12 and 4.3 miles
Time:	1 to 3 hours
Trail Type:	Mixture of singletrack and twotrack
Elevation Gain:	100 to 400 feet
Difficulty:	Difficult for long loop; Family - Easy for short loop
Location:	Ogemaw County
Comments:	Tremendously varied terrain on long loop. The short loop is a great family ride or cruise on flat twotracks.

The Rifle River Recreation Area is a beautiful tract of land that includes the Rifle River, seven lakes, and several creeks. Riding is allowed on most of the hiking trails in the park. The terrain in the park is tremendously varied. The trail around the river is nearly absolutely flat. A great riding opportunity for families and beginners to enjoy themselves. The rolling hills near Grousehaven Lake and Devoe Lake include several grunting climbs and speedy descents. Camping and swimming are available in the park.

The park is located about five miles east of Rose City. The trail for the moderate to difficult ride starts at the modern campground on Grousehaven Lake. Park in the visitor's parking area for the campground. The trail starts on the opposite side of the sandy beach area for the campers. Parking for the easy loop is at the boat launch site for Devoe Lake. Follow the signs to the rustic campground on Devoe Lake. The boat launch area is in the middle of all the campsites.

The easy ride starts at Point 12, which is on the right side of the large meadow that contains the boat launch and playground

equipment. Pass through the beech forest for a short distance
to Point 11. Go left at Point 11 and ride through the large,
grassy meadow. Point 13 is reached as the singletrack
intersects with a twotrack. Read ahead and follow the
description of the ride starting at Point 13.

The difficult ride starts by riding along the west shore of
Grousehaven Lake. Pedal past the boat launch area and drop
down into the beach for the picnic area. Go left into the
parking area for the picnic area and beach. The trail resumes
in the circle drive on the right. After climbing a steep hill to
leave the paved road, the trail forks. Go right. The trail rolls
dramatically before intersecting with a dirt road. Note that the
trail continues across the dirt road. Save this section of trail
for the return journey.

After the intersection, go right onto the dirt road. The road
drops down between Lodge Lake and Grousehaven Lake.
Point 9 is on the left just as the road starts to bend to the right.
Check out the steep hill on the right of Point 9. Go ahead and
burn some excess energy off on that hill, or save it for the
similar climbs that are just ahead on the trail.

After skirting the edge of Lodge Lake, climb two steep hills on
the excellent singletrack. The crest of the second hill offers a
marvelous view of Lodge Lake on the left and Devoe Lake
with all its islands on the right. Drop down the hill before
facing the huge climb on the ride. The trail is superb so drop
down into a granny gear and get those thighs burning.
Excellent challenge! Fly down the hill and roll past a pond
that contains two active beaver lodges. As the trail is winding
through the beech and birch forest, note a trail merging from
the right. The trail returns to this intersection from that trail
on the return journey. This intersection was not marked when

I rode the trail, but should be Point 10. The trail crosses a dirt road, offers a view of Scaup Lake, and passes through a large meadow before arriving at Point 13.

At Point 13, go left on the twotrack. After the twotrack bends right, watch for the trail to resume on the left. The next long section of the trail is exceptionally flat as it passes through river country.

For a short distance the trail is somewhat rough, but improves as it passes along Skunk Creek. Watch for beaver activity along the trail. The trail crosses the creek and a tributary via small bridges. After passing a twotrack and Point 15, the trail forks. The right fork leads to Spruce Campground. Go left.

The trail forks again at Point 17. The left fork leads to Lost Lake and is worth exploring. Go right as the primo singletrack remains flat. Pedal past Point 19 and through a large clearing before reaching the Rifle River. Cross the river via an impressive suspension bridge.

The hardpacked trail remains flat as it crosses Clear Creek and Point 21. For the next couple of miles, the trail is in a large meadow, close to the river. Select one of several beautiful spots and enjoy a snack or picnic lunch.

Too soon the trail crosses the river again. While I was standing on the bridge, I was fortunate enough to spy a mature eagle riding the warm air thermals up and out of sight. After crossing the bridge, go left along the edge of a single row of pines. The twotrack that leads to the bridge services the Ranch Campground. The trail passes through a meadow before reaching a paved road. Go right on the road. Turn left into the boat launch area. This is the start of the easy ride. The trail resumes on the far right.

To return to the start of the big loop, pedal through the thick forest behind the campground to reach Point 11. Go left at this intersection. Leaving Point 11, the terrain tumbles through a series of thrilling descents and climbs. Go left at the "T" intersection and prepare for a fantastic section of riding. In early June the trail was surrounded by the marvelous white trillium wildflower. As the flower matures, the petals turn a beautiful shade of pink.

At the second "T" intersection after leaving Point 11, go left. The trail is at the unmarked intersection I previously described as Point 10. Enjoy some tremendous drops as the trail returns via the hilly section at the start of the ride. Retrace the trail to the crest of the hill above Lodge and Grousehaven Lakes. Go right onto the trail at the crest of the hill. The trail passes through a beautiful hardwood forest before dropping down to the paved circle drive at the picnic area. Retrace the remainder of the trail to the parking area and the trailhead.

34 Pine Haven Recreation Area
Midland County Parks

Type:	Loop
Distance:	3 miles of flats and 3 miles of hills
Time:	30 to 60 minutes
Trail Type:	Mixture of singletrack and twotrack
Elevation Gain:	Less than 100 feet
Difficulty:	Family - Easy to Moderate
Location:	Midland County
Comments:	Pack the bikes, kids and lunch and spend the day cruising on this well marked and maintained trail system.

Pine Haven Recreation Area is a popular cross country ski and mountain biking area. The exceptionally well marked trail system contains a number of short, intersecting loops. Several segments of the trail cross Mud Creek and skirt the shore of the Salt River. Camping and swimming are located nearby in other Midland County parks.

The recreation area is located northwest of Midland. Exit US-10 at West River Road. Go south on West River. Turn right onto Maynard Road. Maynard Road dead ends after 1.75 miles into the parking area for the park. The trail starts at the information center. More riding is available south of Saginaw Road on a rails-to-trails system.

The number of intersecting trails make it impossible to describe the trail system. The riding between US-10 and Mud Creek is flat and easy. All the trails are cut wide and most are hardpacked. All the "blue" or more difficult trails are rideable by everyone. The trails contain one or two drops and climbs. The terrain is slightly steeper on the most difficult trails. When the trails are dry, these hills can be ridden for a great aerobic workout. The area lends itself to spending the day exploring, riding, and picnicking. None of the trails are far from the parking area. Plan on bringing a lunch or snack to extend the riding time.